BACKYARD PONY

BACKYARD
PONY SELECTING AND OWNING A HORSE

BY FREDERICK L. DEVEREUX, JR.
ILLUSTRATED BY SAM SAVITT

FRANKLIN WATTS, INC. | NEW YORK 1975

Library of Congress Cataloging in Publication Data

Devereux, Frederick L   1914–
    Backyard pony.

    Bibliography: p.
    Includes index.
    SUMMARY: Gives instructions on choosing and
caring for a pet pony including information on sta-
bling, feeding, equipment, and training.
    1. Ponies—Juvenile literature. [1. Ponies] I.
Savitt, Sam. II. Title.
SF315.D48   636.1'6   75–5544
ISBN 0–531–02833–X

CONTENTS

6.47 Modern 12-29-75

For CHARLIE *and* STEVE

FOREWORD

This is a "how to do it" guide for the junior rider who wants to take care of his or her own mount, either at home or when participating in pony club rallies, horse shows, trail rides, or any of the many other pleasurable activities that depend on an understanding partnership between pony and rider.

We are not speaking of a pony as merely a small horse, but rather as an equine of any height ridden by a junior. Nor is the scope of the book limited to stable management. Rather the intent is to include all the essential information that a prospective first-time owner needs to know about the nonriding aspects of horsemanship, which includes selection of the pony, an insight into how he thinks, how to transport him, and many other factors in addition to his basic care.

A well-kept, well-conditioned, well-mannered pony is a joy to ride. Unfortunately, one sees today a great number of ponies that are somewhat less than a joy due to the lack of knowledge or carelessness of their young owners—ruined by overfeeding, stumble-footed from bad shoeing, sore-backed by an improperly fitted saddle, sore-legged from overriding, dull-coated from indifferent grooming, sour-dispositioned, head-shy, difficult to load in a trailer—the list is a long one. Misplaced kindness and ignorance of the basic principles of stable management are the principal causes of a pony not performing up to his potential; no matter how skilled the rider may be, it is impossible to derive much pleasure from a pony that has not had the benefits of proper care.

Backyard Pony was written as a result of my pleasant association with several hundred eager and enthusiastic junior riders, all of whom were interested in taking good care of their ponies and few of whom —in this age of urbanization—had the fundamental background knowledge that was a matter of course with their grandparents in the horse and buggy era. It is hoped that this book will help the young owner to understand his or her pony's needs, and how to take care of him, so that the end result will be a happy and enduring partnership of proud owner and willing, healthy pony.

Frederick L. Devereux, Jr.

Woodstock, Vermont
September 1974

I

CHOOSING THE RIGHT PONY

Three major considerations when buying a pony are the checkbook balance, the pony's suitability to the rider, and the main purpose for which the pony is to be used. Since the perfectly made, perfectly mannered pony has yet to be born, any purchase is a compromise with the ideal. A pony should be considered to be a long-term investment and his selection should not be made in haste; one should look at a number of prospects before narrowing the choice.

Cost is not solely a matter of how much (or how little) can be spent. Considerable savings may be made, depending on the use to which the pony will be put, if the buyer is willing to overlook some minor defects and forego some of the nonessential niceties such as color, height, and breed papers. If the objective is major horse show or combined training competition, be prepared to spend top dollar. If, on the other hand, the pony is wanted purely as a pleasure mount for country trail riding, it may be possible to find a more than adequate one at a price well under the budget ceiling. It is important to bear in mind the purpose for which the pony is wanted, otherwise one is likely to wind up with—and pay a premium for—more pony than is needed.

Some knowledge of conformation (appearance, structure, and proportion) is essential. If the buyer is not already a keen student of conformation, he or she should obtain the services of a knowledgeable friend or professional horseman. An elementary knowledge will en-

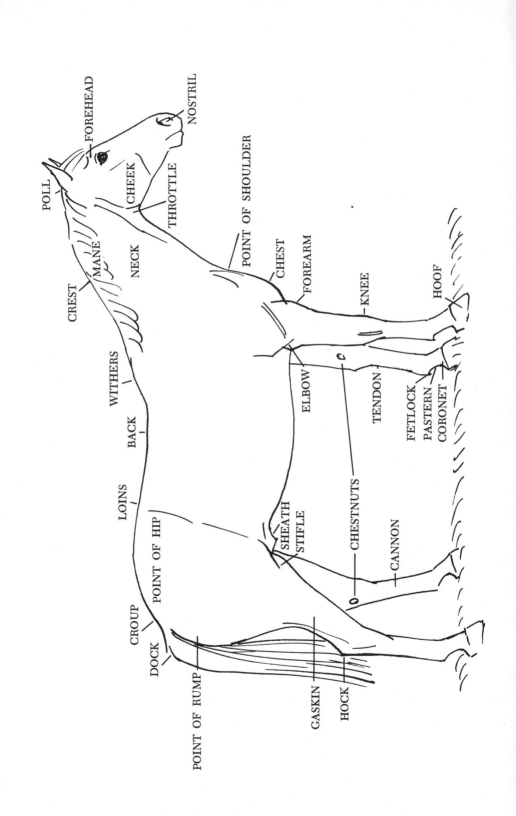

able the prospective buyer to weed out most of the undesirables and concentrate on the final options. At this point the best expert judgment should be solicited. As a beginning, therefore, the buyer should be reasonably familiar with the points of a pony.

A knowledge of the leading breeds, and their capabilities or special attributes, is helpful if the pony is intended to do specialized work such as hunting, jumping, endurance rides, or horse show equitation. The true pony breeds most commonly found include:

Shetland. Smallest of the pony breeds, with compact body, short legs, thick coat, and dense mane and tail. They are clever, docile when unspoiled, and friendly. An excellent weight carrier, the Shetland's principal faults are a broad back (difficult for a short-legged rider to sit properly) and a thick, short neck which a willful pony uses to resist the rider's attempts to guide him with the reins. Shetlands rarely jump very high or wide.

Connemara. A useful, all-purpose breed but not a very pretty one. Good disposition combined with courage and excellent jumping ability make this Irish pony an ideal small hunter or junior three-day-event mount.

Welsh. Closely resembles a small horse, with more of a quality look than most pony breeds. A good jumper, likely to be somewhat more spirited than the Shetland or Connemara. Takes well to harness and is a popular driving pony.

Other pony breeds include the *hackney,* essentially a harness type and likely to have a very rough trot for riding purposes. Nervous and sensitive, but willing under the hands of a skilled rider or driver, the hackney is definitely not a good beginner's mount. *Exmoor, Dartmoor,* and *New Forest* ponies are well established in Britain; they are small, rugged, independent types. The best ones make excellent mounts but are hard to find. The *Pony of the Americas* is a Western type with Appaloosa (spotted) markings. He makes a good trail horse and is becoming a popular mount in horse shows, particularly in the West and Midwest.

The breeds of horses suitable for a junior rider include:

Arabian. Oldest of the established breeds, with great intelligence, courage, and disposition. The Arabian is close-coupled (short-backed) and a rather small animal when compared to the other horse breeds. Arabians have good speed (they were the original racehorses) and moderate jumping ability. The gaits, particularly the trot, are smooth and flowing. A popular cross for producing superior children's hunters is the Arabian/Welsh pony. The purebred Arabian is likely to be a little too much horse for the beginning rider, but is an excellent mount for the more experienced junior. Unfortunately the rapidly increasing popularity of the breed has resulted in the production of some misfits with fat "mutton" withers (difficult to keep the saddle in place) and a condition called "cow hocks" in which the points of the hocks turn inward. If severe, this can cause interference with the hind legs.

Morgan. A famous American breed of utility horse, suitable for riding or driving. Morgans tend to be on the small side, making them quite suitable for young riders. The typical Morgan has a fast walk, a good trot, and a barely adequate canter. His disposition is unexcelled, particularly if he is of the original Justin Morgan type and has not been overly infused with saddlebred blood. The true Morgan type is blocky, muscular, and docile, with short legs. Seldom found out hunting or competing where speed at the gallop is important, the Morgan's true forte is in pleasure riding and driving on country roads. Crossbreeding with the Arabian has not been successful.

Tennessee walker or *plantation* horse. Those that have not been abused for horse show purposes are quiet, with a big, ground-covering, running walk. They dislike the canter and are not sufficiently handy for an all-purpose children's mount, but are ideal for comfortable country riding.

Saddlebred. This three- and five-gaited beauty is popular at horse shows and noted for his high-stepping trot. Saddlebreds make surprisingly good mounts, provided the disposition is sufficiently placid. With feet properly trimmed, the action is not as exaggerated as in the show ring; the use of a mild bit, so that the horse is not afraid of the rider's hands, encourages better balance. The breed is not suited for jumping and is not sufficiently rugged for extended hard work cross-country.

Standardbred. The sulky-pulling trotting (or pacing) horse of the raceways can be a very uncomfortable ride, but his disposition is good and he is an easy keeper. Crosses with Arabians and thoroughbreds have produced some outstanding hunters and hacks.

Quarter horse. So called for his great speed at short distances, the muscular quarter horse has become deservedly popular as an all-purpose hack—practically panic-proof and willing to try anything. It is an ideal type for a home stable where versatility and good sense are more important than ability at a specialization such as show ring jumping, dressage, or any of the other mounted activities that require acrobatic training. A good, not overly large or too thick-shouldered quarter horse is hard to beat as a junior's mount.

Thoroughbred. With more heart, more speed, more spirit, and more nervousness than any other breed, the thoroughbred is not for the novice rider. An infusion of thoroughbred blood improves any breed of light horse and a part-thoroughbred is much sought after by those riders who want something more than cold blood, but not the high-strung qualities which set this breed apart. A cross of thoroughbred with Morgan, saddlebred, standardbred, or quarter horse often produces a superior junior mount, particularly if the thoroughbred's conformation and way of moving are transmitted in conjunction with the other breed's disposition and more rugged bone. Some thoroughbred blood is almost mandatory if the rider wishes to fox hunt, undertake serious dressage work, or exhibit in the leading horse shows.

Very probably, the breeding will be "unknown" with most juniors' ponies, and it will take an experienced eye to determine the mix of breeds in the pony's ancestry. These ponies are often the most useful of all, except for specialized competitive purposes: they require minimum care, are accustomed to fending for themselves, and combine hardiness and stamina with quiet dispositions. Breeding has little to do with the primary requirements of safety, surefootedness, and common sense which are of paramount concern when selecting a junior's mount.

In selecting a mount, the following factors should be considered luxuries—nice to have but not essential:

Height costs money. A thoroughbred children's hunter standing 16½ hands (a hand is 4 inches) will sell for a thousand dollars more than his 4-inch-shorter full brother, yet height has little or nothing to do with weight-carrying ability. Furthermore, the shorter animal will in all probability be a more agile athlete, better able to get out of a tight spot safely. Jumping ability is in no way related to height.

Color costs money if it happens to be gray, chestnut, or Appaloosa spots. These colors can command a premium of a hundred dollars or more as compared to the same quality of a bay, brown, black, or pinto. A gray, in particular, is an abomination to groom and keep clean, and the logic of the situation would seem to demand that grays should sell at a discount. However, horse and pony trading is seldom based on much logic, as the buyer soon discovers.

Breed papers cost money for the obvious reasons. A horse or pony sold without papers always goes for a lower price. If a guarantee of breeding is not important to the buyer for showing or breeding purposes, there is little reason for insisting on papers.

Sex can be expensive, since stallions and mares have breeding potential. A stallion is usually too rank, or spirited, for a junior to work around safely and mares are likely to get very touchy when in heat, which occurs every three weeks or so. A gelding, on the other hand, will sell at a lower price and usually does not present the temperamental problems found in the sexed animals.

Where to look for a suitable pony or small horse depends somewhat upon the facilities in the area in which you live. If a definite breed is under consideration and a breeding farm is within traveling distance, this is usually the best bet, particularly if a young animal is desired. For most of us, however, breeding farms are either too remote, the prices are likely to be too high, or we want a well-broken mount with a little more age on him than the young stock the farm has to offer. A reputable dealer is the logical next step. Contrary to the legends one hears about dealers, most of them are reputable; a horse and pony dealer knows that a good reputation is money in the bank. Furthermore, even if he may not have just exactly what you are looking for in his barn at the time of your visit, he will probably know where to lay hands on it; dealers know their territory.

A reputable dealer will not lie to you, but you must ask the right questions rather than expect him to volunteer information that might tend to lessen the selling price. The first question should be, "Is this pony sound?" (A sound pony is free from disease and serious defects.) The smart dealer will answer, "Yes, in my opinion." The second question then becomes, "Will you put that in writing?" If the answer is an equivocation, beware—or at least call in a veterinarian before passing any money. And never buy from a dealer if he will not give you a trial period before the purchase becomes final.

Very often the local public stable, or "riding academy," will have a pony that can be tried out for suitability before making an offer. You can expect the pony to have a bit of age ("long in the tooth") and, if he is really earning his keep, the owner may not be interested in selling. If the stable does not have an indoor riding ring, and the locale is in the snow belt, an offer made in late fall might be accepted, whereas it would have been turned down flat in the springtime.

Camp ponies come on the market about Labor Day, when the season ends. As with public stables in the North, camp proprietors are faced with the cost of keeping animals over a long, unproductive winter. Many camps are willing to lend ponies (or lease for a pittance) to responsible riders during the off season.

Auctions of horses in training are held periodically at the racetracks. If a horse is being sold at auction simply because it has the "slows" and is a nonwinner, it may turn out to be a real bargain as a hunter. However, many of the animals coming under the auctioneer's hammer at the track are there for leg or wind problems, so a veterinarian examination is advisable before bidding. A horse fresh off the track must be "let down" or "unwound" and reschooled for pleasure riding—a large order for a junior rider with limited experience.

A good place to stay away from is the weekly auction advertising "a carload of fresh horses just in from the West." West, in this frame of reference, may be a few miles in any direction. The carload (if it exists at all) will be supplemented by castoffs of every description, many of them doctored up to pass a superficial examination for soundness. There is no guarantee of wind, eyesight, sound legs, or freedom from disease, and no recourse once the buyer's bid has been accepted.

Buying at a weekly auction is a risky business, truly a case of "let the buyer beware."

There remains the private owner who, for one reason or another, has a pony to sell. One of two rationales is always given: either the rider has outgrown the pony or else the rider is going away to school. While either or both may be true, it is wise to search out other reasons, particularly if there are other juniors in the family who are the right size and still going to school in the neighborhood. The classified advertising sections and the sports pages of metropolitan and regional newspapers are good sources of information on ponies being offered at private sale, as is *The Chronicle of the Horse*, a weekly paper published in Middleburg, Virginia, and generally regarded as the leading horse publication in the country.

The general tone of the seller's stable is a good indication of the kind of treatment his livestock receives. If the stable is unkempt and foul smelling, one should suspect that care has not been of the best; the pony may not have been fed properly, his feet and coat may have been neglected, and he may be nervous or bad-tempered as a result of inconsiderate handling. A pony seen in such surroundings should be given a careful examination for incipient disease and permanent deterioration of muscle, bone, sight, and digestive and respiratory systems. On the other side of the coin, a pony found in a "gold plated" stable, and accustomed to the best of stabling, feed, and care, can also be a problem. If you are not prepared to give him much the same treatment in your own stable he will fall off a bit in condition and not thereafter be quite the same pony; this is particularly true of animals with a good proportion of thoroughbred blood.

When the time comes for a close inspection, it is best to follow an orderly routine. First of all, make a point of seeing the pony at rest in his stall. Observe the walls. If the wood has been chewed he may be a cribber. Does he stand quietly, or does he flinch or resist the groom entering his stall? Does he stand quietly to be tacked up, or is he perhaps head-shy? When he is ready to be brought out make haste to precede him, and watch as he comes through the door into the daylight; hesitation can be a sign of defective eyesight. Have him brought to a point about twenty feet away from you and watch him in a relaxed, natural stance, with all four feet on the ground. If at this point he displeases your eye for any reason—consciously or purely as a matter of undefined instinct—it is best to reject him; he will never please you completely, and it will not be a satisfactory partnership. Assuming that he does pass your test of general acceptance thus far, observe how he stands. A pointed foreleg is a sign of soreness, or even the serious navicular disease. Is he alert, but standing quietly on a loose rein, or is the groom jigging him and holding his head up? Is he

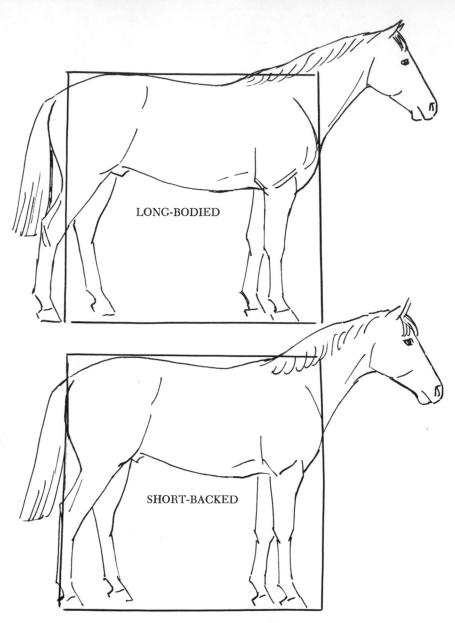

LONG-BODIED

SHORT-BACKED

short-backed, the sign of handiness (agility) and easy keeping, or is he rangy with a long body that will always look underfed? Are his legs well under him? Are his pasterns set at a comfortable (about 35 degrees) angle? If too vertical, they will not act properly as shock absorbers; if too sloping ("coon-footed"), they may be too weak for jumping or hard work. Is the tail carried proudly (a sign of good health) or is it drooping? Is the head too large in proportion to the neck and is the neck too short in proportion to the body? A heavy-headed, thick-necked pony, if willful, can be hard to hold.

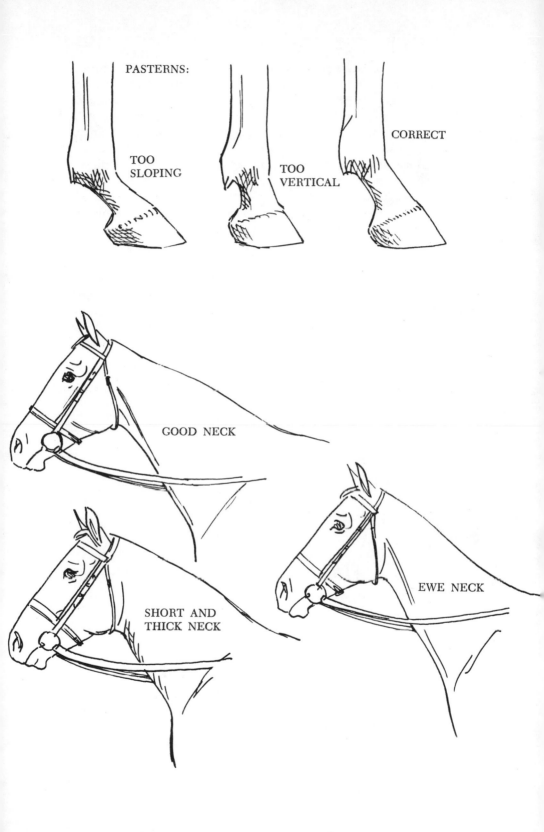

PASTERNS:

TOO SLOPING

TOO VERTICAL

CORRECT

GOOD NECK

SHORT AND THICK NECK

EWE NECK

Note that we have made no mention of two physical features that get high priority from conformation judges: shoulder and top line. If the saddle fits properly, and there is no feeling of riding downhill when the pony is tried under saddle a little later on, the top line will be satisfactory, even if not a symmetrical perfection. As to the shoulder, it slopes beautifully in the thoroughbred and Arabian, and is more nearly vertical in the standardbred; if the pony moves well, and is comfortable at the trot and canter, it will be acceptable. Similarly, no mention has been made of the bottom line in this suggested observation routine; the herring-gutted or tightly drawn belly will be apparent at first observation because it offends the eye. Such a bottom line is obviously a difficult configuration to keep a saddle from slipping backward.

After the profile viewing, walk to the rear of the pony. Does one hip drop when he is standing on all fours? Are the hind legs "split up the middle" and therefore weak and wobbly at the walk? Are both hocks the same size and not enlarged? Is the pony cow-hocked (hocks tending to point in toward each other)? Cow hocks limit thrust, and thus cut down on speed and jumping ability.

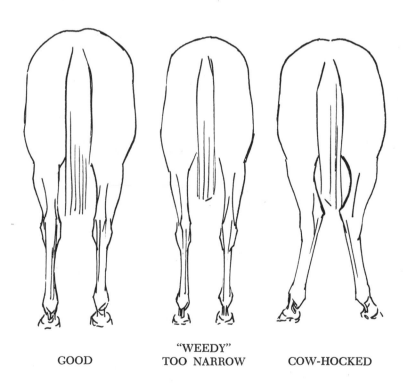

GOOD   "WEEDY"   COW-HOCKED
        TOO NARROW

Now walk in front of the pony. Is there ample room in the chest for heart and lungs, or do the legs "come out of the same hole"? Are both knees the same size and not enlarged (a big knee can be a sign of a bad fall and indicate a permanent weakness, though it can also result from a minor injury)? Are both forefeet the same size and in proportion—neither too small nor too large—to the legs? Is the eye prominent without bulging? For some reason, perhaps because of impaired vision, ponies with sunken eyes tend to have bad manners. Finally step to the side of the head and rather swiftly sweep the hand close to, but behind, the pony's eye. He should blink; if not, suspect blindness. If you have memorized an equine dental chart, you may want now to inspect the mouth for age. However, at this stage of the game—and particularly if you are unsure of yourself—the better part of wisdom is merely to ask. The dishonest owner may well have had the teeth "bishoped" (filed down); the honest owner will tell you. Briefly, a pony does not get a full set of teeth before the age of five. At about the ninth year *Galvayne's groove* appears close to the gums on the upper incisor teeth and extends gradually downward for the next ten years. The front teeth of a young pony are oblong, in middle age they become round, and finally, in old age, triangular when viewed toward the chewing surface.

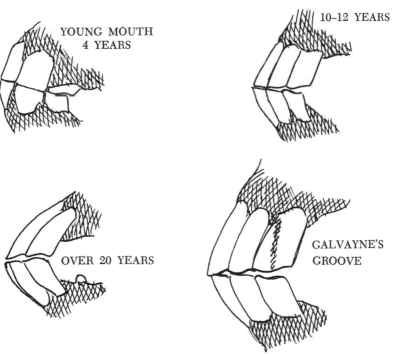

YOUNG MOUTH
4 YEARS

10–12 YEARS

OVER 20 YEARS

GALVAYNE'S
GROOVE

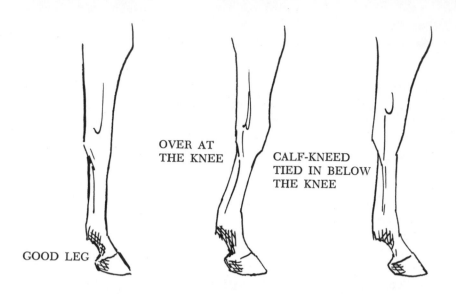

OVER AT
THE KNEE

CALF-KNEED
TIED IN BELOW
THE KNEE

GOOD LEG

Now to check the legs and feet at close range, for the saying, "no foot, no horse" is unquestionably true. Is the pony calf-kneed, or "tied in" below the knee? Both are serious defects. Less serious, but not to be entirely discounted, is being "over at the knee," a condition which may lead to a fall when landing after a jump.

Run both hands simultaneously down the cannons of each foreleg. If one feels warmer than the other, however slight the difference, the pony is not sound. Perhaps rest will effect a cure but a veterinarian should make the final judgment. At the same time test the tendons for elasticity. Inflexibility is a sign of past injury, which should make the purchase questionable. Pick up the feet and inspect the frog; it should be soft and unshriveled. A healthy frog touches the ground, a hard frog with a shrunken, dull appearance indicates serious foot trouble.

GOOD FOOT

CONTRACTED HEEL
SHRIVELED FROG

Assuming the pony so far has passed your somewhat elementary inspection, ask to have him trotted away from you, turned sharply, and trotted back. Insist that this be done on a loose halter shank. A shrewd groom can conceal the nodding that indicates the pony's lameness by holding the head up. A hard surface, either an impacted dirt driveway or a hard-topped road, should be used for this test. Look for a smooth trot, not choppy, with the head steady. Does the pony paddle, toeing in and splaying his forelegs outward much as a girl runs in a tight skirt? If so, he will lack speed. Toeing out is even less desirable. Do his hind legs move well, without wobbling, when viewed from directly behind? Does he tend to overreach, or grab a front shoe with his hind shoe? Is there an even cadence to the beat of the feet?

At this point, the buyer should have a fairly good impression of the pony's desirability from the standpoint of soundness. Unless there is definite interest there is little point in wasting more time. On the other hand, if the pony pleases the eye, and his defects are not of a serious nature, he should now be tried under saddle.

The pony should fit the rider, a too-small pony being much more of a liability than one slightly too large. If the rider is still growing, a somewhat oversized pony will be useful for a longer period. The test of size in relation to rider is to determine where the rider's feet are positioned when in the stirrup irons. The heel should fall close to, but not below, the bottom line of the pony's chest.

It is desirable that the pony's prospective rider, if reasonably experienced, should be in the saddle for the final mounted tests. If the pony is being considered for a novice, then some qualified rider must be substituted. The rider should take the reins and ask the groom to stand back in order to see if the pony will stand quietly to be mounted. Next the pony should be put into a sharp trot on a hard surface, halted, and asked to back. The number of ponies that will not stand to be mounted and are difficult to back is surprisingly large. While they can be taught to perform these basic functions by the new owner, their lack can be used as a bargaining point on the asking price.

Assuming the pony has trotted out sound, without the telltale nodding of the head that indicates lameness, he should be put into a brisk gallop of several hundred yards as a test of wind. If the pony is in good condition and not too fat, his flanks should not heave after this mild workout; if they do heave in spasms, he has respiratory problems. A better method, which takes practice and experience, is to place one's ear against his side and listen for the sounds of spastic breathing. A few snorts to clear the nostrils, particularly at the beginning of the gallop, are of no consequence, but labored noisy breathing is cause for rejection. The gait should be a true gallop, not a collected canter.

The final mounted test is for general handiness. If the pony is sound, and well-made, the amount of his schooling will largely determine the price. Depending on what stage of training is desired (do you want to school the pony at home, or do you need a finished product?), he should be ridden according to the use for which he is wanted, for example, over fences if he is to hunt or jump.

The final test for a junior's mount—far more important than conformation, soundness, or schooling—is *manners*, the paramount requirement. Make certain of his disposition—a nervous, kicking, or biting pony will surely spoil the young rider's enjoyment and may well sour him or her on riding as a recreational activity. On the other hand, the joys afforded by a well-mannered pony will more than compensate for minor conformation defects or a slight stiffness at the beginning of a ride. It is impossible to love an ill-mannered beast, and the love of a child for his or her mount is an important part of the relationship between rider and pony.

II

UNDERSTANDING THE PONY

A pony's intelligence and reasoning power are quite limited; they are much less than a dog's but considerably more than a cow's. He does, however, have an excellent memory. He is a creature of habit; when the habits please us, he is termed well-mannered; when they cause displeasure he is called ill-mannered, sour, stubborn, and lots of other uncomplimentary words. Some of a pony's habits are hereditary. For example, he wants to run away when frightened; but most of his habits are a result of the way he is trained and treated by humans. Therefore it is very important to understand the basic nature of the pony—why he acts as he does, how he reacts to situations, and how to overcome instinctive habits (such as the desire to run away when frightened) by training him properly to obey his master rather than his instinct.

First of all, one should know a little about the pony's heredity and how he evolved from a timid little forest creature into man's most useful animal servant. All ponies and horses descend from *Eohippus*, a creature about the size of a fox, who roamed the forests about 500 million years ago. Eohippus was a browser, eating the leaves of trees and plants. He had many enemies among the flesh-eating animals, such as the saber-toothed tiger; thus he became a fast runner to escape being eaten. Since the race for life belongs to the swift, only the fastest survived. Over many centuries, Eohippus grew longer and

longer legs (and a correspondingly larger body to keep them far enough apart and supplied with sufficient blood and oxygen) as he gradually developed into a very fast runner. In time, Eohippus moved from the forest to the plains and became a grazer (a grass-eater) rather than a leaf-eater, since grass was plentiful and trees were scarce. Different enemies were found on the plains—lions, cheetahs, and leopards—and Eohippus found a new defense weapon to fend them off, his hooves. If he could not run from his enemies (who were faster than he over short distances), he could kick them with his long legs. These two defenses from danger, flight and kicking when in close quarters, are very strong in the heredity of today's pony; they are instinctive habits which must be modified by intelligent and understanding handling.

Eohippus needed to spot his enemies from far off, and nature therefore gave him good long-range eyesight but neglected to provide good close-up vision, which is why a pony may stumble over a low log immediately in front of him if he is not allowed to put his head down and a bit to the side to examine it as he approaches the obstacle. And nature also placed the eyes on each side of the head so that they can move independently of each other and cover a full 360 degrees of observation. Since Eohippus needed to observe movement, rather than color, his perception was in black and white, with most of what he saw being a shade of gray. His descendant, the pony, sees in the same way; in other words he is color-blind. So we must remember that the pony sees objects much differently than humans do and, because of his instinct for survival, strange and light-colored objects may tend to frighten him until he has become accustomed to them.

As a grazer on the open plains, Eohippus was constantly on the alert against predatory enemies, hence he ate little, but often, grabbing a mouthful of grass and then spending much time searching the horizon for danger. As a consequence, today's pony has inherited a very small stomach relative to his size; he is much better off when fed small quantities at frequent intervals. When a pony's stomach becomes overfull, he is subject to much more severe internal distress than a human is after overeating. The proper feeding of a pony, both as to content and amount, is a prime responsibility of the person taking care of him.

Another distinctive characteristic of the pony is the ability to sleep standing up. Sleeping on his feet saved Eohippus time in taking off when danger approached, and was made possible by the development of a system of tendons and ligaments which take the weight strain off the muscles and bones. Old ponies, fearful of not having the strength to get up, often spend the last several years of life on their feet. Standing ponies frequently catch forty winks, and it is impossible to tell from behind whether a relaxed pony is asleep or awake.

To avoid being kicked by a suddenly awakening pony, whose instinct tells him he is being attacked from the rear, it is a wise precaution to speak to him as you approach from behind.

As with all animals, the pony's sense of smell is far better developed than that of humans. This causes him to shy at times to the complete mystification of his rider. As riders of mountain trails are aware, a pony will panic at the smell of a far-off bear, or even at stale bear scent on the trail. Since the pony considers the bear to be his natural enemy, anything he smells that reminds him of danger will cause unrest. You may never ride your pony in bear country, but you very probably will at some time be in the vicinity of pigs and notice the pony beginning to fidget and show signs of wanting to leave the area; his concern is caused by the pig odor, which closely resembles that of bear. This similarity is not surprising, considering that both the pig and bear belong to the same family.

The pony's hearing is also more acute than that of his rider, and an unfamiliar sound, which the rider may not hear, will make him tensely alert. The rider who recognizes that an unfamiliar sound (or a smell believed to emanate from a dangerous source) is the cause of the pony's unrest will make the proper corrections—by voice and leg aids —to soothe the pony and dominate him. On the other hand, the rider who does not understand the pony's timidity is likely to make one of two errors: either assume that the pony is "spooky" and therefore dangerous, or else to treat him cruelly by overpunishment.

It is often seen that a "doggy" pony, that is, one who is overly placid and quiet when being hacked, will wake up and be quite animated in the hunting field. Ponies are excited by seeing motion, another throwback to the wild days when the sight of a galloping herd was a sign of escape from danger. Since ponies are gregarious by instinct, and prefer to be part of a group or herd rather than being alone, they tend to follow the crowd and are more at ease in the company of other ponies than when stabled, pastured, or ridden alone. Young ponies will behave better and be less flighty when in the company of older, more sedate animals. Horsemen utilize this characteristic in training green ponies; whenever possible they should be taught their lessons in company with well-mannered ponies. However, catering to a pony's liking for company can be overdone, for a pony accustomed to be at all times with other ponies may become herdbound and very reluctant to be ridden alone. Therefore the judicious trainer will want to school the pony in company in order to teach him calmness, but at times will work him alone to ensure that the herd instinct is overcome.

Similarly, the question is often raised whether ponies understand the human voice, and the evidence here is positive. Words are not understood but the tone of voice definitely is. Inflection is important; a sharp tone will animate the pony and a soft, dragged-out, lowering inflection will soothe him. The voice, properly used, is an important aid in controlling a pony. Cavalry troop horses quickly learned that an increase in gait was called for when they heard, for example, "Trot, Ho!" uttered sharply by the unit commander; a softer "Waaalk Hooo" was the signal to decrease the gait. Many ponies can be taught to come to the pasture gate at the sound of a whistle, provided there is reward in the form of a handful of grain or a carrot or other delicacy, an example of the association of ideas which is basic to all animal training.

The pony's excellent memory makes him adaptable to learning the lessons that are taught to him. This attribute can be a mixed blessing if the pony is not handled intelligently; for example, if he hits his head on a low-roofed trailer, he will remember that loading on a trailer hurts and may be reluctant to enter any trailer in the future, no matter how generous the headroom. Or, if he should be bridled carelessly, so that the buckle rubs his eye, he may become permanently head-shy when his handler attempts to bridle or halter him. Certainly he will remember which humans he can trust to handle him humanely and intelligently—and for these handlers he will perform willingly. On the other hand, he also remembers those who abuse him, or mishandle him out of ignorance, and their reward will be a less-willing, recalcitrant pony.

To summarize: The pony, by heredity, is a timid creature whose instinct is to avoid danger—real or assumed—by flight. If he cannot flee, he will kick to protect himself. He can be easily startled. He has highly developed senses of hearing and smell and is therefore aware of many environmental factors which escape humans. He sees things much differently than do humans. His digestive system is a delicate one, and he is subject to severe illness if improperly fed when stabled. His intelligence is limited but he has an excellent memory. He is a creature of habit, the habits being shaped both by his heredity and by the way man handles and trains him. Where instinct conflicts with training, the intelligence, patience, and understanding of his master determine whether the pony will be well mannered or not. A pony is a reflection of his owner/rider; the pony of a considerate and knowledgeable junior is easily handled, gentle, willing, and trusting, whereas the pony of an inconsiderate owner proves the adage that a pony's faults are man-made.

III

STABLING AND PASTURE

Wild ponies seek shelter only from strong winds; cold, snow, and rain do not make them uncomfortable to any significant extent. The domesticated pony living year round on pasture is likely to be far healthier and hardier than his stable-kept brother, provided he has adequate food and water and a good windbreak. A stable actually is a device for man's convenience in the management of horseflesh, rather than a humane improvement over the animal's natural habitat. The best stabling is that which most nearly accommodates the pony's natural life-style.

Ponies are successfully kept in chicken coops, garages, tool sheds, and cowbarns as well as in conventional stables. If you plan to convert an existing structure to house a pony, certain requirements for comfort, health, and safety must be borne in mind. Concrete flooring, such as found in a garage or cow barn, is an abomination and should be removed. Concrete is slippery, injurious to the feet, and requires an inordinate amount of bedding to induce the pony to lie down. The best stall flooring is tamped clay over crushed rock or drain tile; when properly packed, it requires little maintenance. Next best is a dirt floor (remove topsoil and use the hardpan). If a wooden floor is to be left intact for a stall installation, it must be composed of heavy planks, otherwise it is best to rip it out before the pony has a chance to damage the floor and probably injure himself in the process. Ideally, stall floors

should have a gentle slope (about 1 inch per 3 feet) for drainage toward the aisle.

Ponies do better in a loose box stall than when tied in a straight stall. The minimum size box stall for a small pony should be at least 8′ × 8′, for a large pony 10′ × 10′, and for a horse 12′ × 12′. If possible, enlarge these dimensions by adding 2 feet to one side. It is false economy to build small stalls. The wear and tear on the floors will be severe, cleaning out the stall while the pony is occupying it will be difficult, and the cramped conditions will affect the pony's well-being and thus fatten the veterinarian's bankroll. If a straight stall must be used, it should be at least 4 feet wide and 8 feet deep. Stall doors should be at least 4 feet wide and of the Dutch type, that is, in two sections, opening independently of each other. If they are interior, opening on an aisle, the top half should be constructed of mesh wire for visibility. Stall doors should always open out, or slide; an inward-swinging door can cause injury. Ponies are very clever at opening latches with their lips and teeth; therefore it is essental to use a foolproof door latch. Stall walls should be substantial, 2″ × 12″ planks, preferably oak, kick proof, and sufficiently sturdy. If tongue and groove planking is used, a tight fit with no warping is ensured. The planks should be dropped into vertical framing—loose, not fastened with nails—so that they may be removed in case of emergency. Walls between stalls should be high enough to divert drafts from the pony's back, but not so high that he cannot see his neighbor in the adjoining stall. In order to provide both visibility and protection, wire mesh should be installed over the stall wall as an extension of the side, rising high enough so that the pony cannot get his head above it even when standing on his hind feet; this mesh should be of the heavy industrial type; chicken coop wire will not last overnight.

The choice of bedding will depend on what is locally available. Peat moss is unquestionably superior; it is absorbent and soft. It is also expensive, even though long-lasting. Wheat straw is highly satisfactory. In some areas wood shavings are available at low cost and are excellent provided they are screened to eliminate chips and sharp fragments. Sawdust is economical but can easily become fly-blown, irritates the skin if damp, and is a fire hazard. Old moldy hay should never be used; the pony will attempt to eat it and severe gastrointestinal disorder will result.

Storage space for bedding, hay, grain, supplies, and equipment depends on space available and may be quite a problem. If hay must be stored overhead, it should always be baled; loose hay is subject to combustion and is a definite fire hazard. Grain, bran, and similar feeds should be in rat-proof containers; galvanized garbage cans with secure tops are ideal and inexpensive. An area outside the building must be reserved for manure until it can be carted away.

Ventilation and light are important to the pony's health. Although drafts should be avoided, free circulation of air should be provided. A window set high in the stall is highly desirable. It should be covered with wire on the inside, and so installed that rain will not enter the stall through the opening. This can be accomplished by hinging it at the bottom and allowing it to open inward about 30 degrees. An electric light can be helpful at night, for evening feeding or other late chores. Open flames, cigarette smoking, or kerosene lanterns should not be allowed in a stable, nor should the stable ever be heated (except, perhaps, the tack room).

As discussed in detail in the chapter on feeding, most true ponies require little or no grain. However, provision should be made for a feed bucket—even if it is only to be used for a bran mash—to be placed in a corner of the stall and secured by snap hooks. A water bucket should be placed in the opposite corner, also secured by snap hooks. Better than a water bucket, but more expensive, is a permanent water bubbler drinking fountain which the pony will quickly learn to activate whenever he is thirsty. A permanent holder for salt bricks should be installed near the water corner. A hay manger is not recommended; it can be injurious to the pony's knees and sides. Feed hay from the floor and forget about mangers or nets. Hay nets must be placed high, and cause eye injury from dust and small stalks. Remember that in the wild state the pony grazes from the ground.

If starting from scratch to build a stable, locate it about fifty yards from the house and downwind (from the prevailing wind) from the house on level ground. In most parts of the country this will be eastward from the house. A southerly exposure is desirable, which means that the main axis of the building will run approximately east to west. Suitable materials include clapboard, plywood with battens, or concrete block. Shingle construction on the side walls is not recommended, nor is cinder block. A brick exterior is excellent, but expensive because of labor costs. A permanent foundation is best, tending to be more rat proof, durable, and providing a tight juncture with the ground level. Pole construction is adequate if proper footings are provided, but will require more maintenance and is subject to flooding from heavy rains. Nothing is more disconcerting than having the stall walls awash from water running in under the sides of the stable. Wood may be left bare on the outside, to weather over the years; after a decade or so it will lose its raw look and blend in with the landscape. Paint or stain will generally prove more pleasing to the eye, and a creosote-base stain is undoubtedly the best wood preservative. All

interior woodwork that the pony can reach with his teeth should be creosoted. A white creosote base stain has recently come on the market and appears to be a happy, low-maintenance solution for those who would otherwise prefer white paint.

The final requirement for a pony's comfort and peace of mind in stable is companionship. A herd creature by instinct, he is restless when penned up alone. Catering to his desire for companionship will reduce stall walking, stall kicking, and pawing, and the mental depression engendered by loneliness. If the stable is to contain more than one pony, then there will be no problem unless one is too domineering. But many a pony has been made happy and content with a dog, goat, or bantam rooster for company. Make provision for a stablemate.

A pony cannot be kept continuously healthy in a stall. On mornings or afternoons when he is not to be ridden, he should be turned out for self-exercise. For this purpose a small paddock adjacent to the stable is needed, with water available; an old bathtub will serve ideally for this purpose, but should be drained daily. Too large a paddock will present difficulties in catching the pony; too small an area will quickly become cut up by hooves and degenerate into a mud pile. An area of approximately 1000 square feet ($100' \times 100'$) should be suitable for a single pony, with an extra 500 feet added for each additional occupant. The paddock should not be used for a grazing area and is not a substitute for pasture.

Pasture, if available, is very beneficial to the pony's health and an important means of saving on hay bills during the green season. A pony at pasture, particularly if the pasture has a tree in it, should be brought into the stable during thunderstorms. The rain will bother him very little, but the danger of being struck by lightning is ever-present. Do not turn out the pony on fresh pasture until the grass has had a chance to mature, and turn him out only for a short period of time the first two weeks after a long winter on hay, otherwise he will scour (get diarrhea) and fall off in condition. Most true ponies, unless undergoing extremely hard daily work, will get along very well on grass alone as a feed. Horses will require a grain supplement. A discussion of grass will be found in the following chapter, which is devoted to the feeding of ponies.

The fencing of paddocks and pastures is best done with wood, either post and rail or post and plank. Locust posts will last practically forever, but are hard to find in many parts of the country. Chestnut, also becoming scarce, is next best. With the exception of locust, which seems to be impervious to rot, all post sections below ground level should be thoroughly soaked with creosote or some other treatment against rot. Three rails or planks are the minimum number that should be used—four are better. If planks are used instead of rails they should

(27)

be substantial (2" × 12" is ideal) and fastened to the *inside* of the post. Admittedly, the fencing will look prettier to the passerby along the road if the planking is on the outside because it presents a smoother appearance, but this construction is weaker. Ponies and horses lean on fences and at times may panic and try to run through them: planks fastened to the outside of the post will be carried away, whereas planks fastened to the inside will have to be shattered before giving way.

Post and rail fencing should be left to weather naturally, without paint. Post and plank fencing may be left natural, painted, or stained. However, once painted, the fencing must be repainted every other year or so. This is a tedious chore, and a strong argument against painting in the first place.

In recent years the cost of wood fencing has risen astronomically to the point where its use to enclose a large pasture may present a prohibitive expense. The only alternative is wire, a poor substitute at best, since ponies will injure themselves on it sooner or later, unless the wire is carefully installed and periodically inspected and repaired. Barbed wire should never be used when building a fence for ponies or horses—they will lean on it and suffer cuts. Worse still, they will find a soft spot where the tension is slack and entangle themselves. If an existing barbed wire pasture must be used, it should be given a top rail of wood plank. This will help to reduce the hazards. Strong mesh wire, the type used to protect industrial buildings against trespassers, is safer than other wires and should be laced to pipes at top and bottom. This construction, while not as expensive as wood, is still far from cheap. Agricultural wire, the type used to fence cows, is intersected about every 6 inches and thus a pony can easily put a foot through the opening and injure himself attempting to withdraw it. This wire, however, is used widely in backyard pony pastures because of its low cost. Its major disadvantages, the open mesh and weak top, can be compensated for by running an electric wire (commonly called an electric *fence*) around the pasture about two feet from the inside of the agricultural wire.

By far the least expensive means of fencing a pasture is to use the electric wire alone, without any back-up fence at all.

Ponies must be taught to respect an electric fence. After all, a single strand of wire in a large field is not a very formidable-looking restraint. Left to his own devices, an exuberant pony at play might easily run through the wire when first turned into the pasture and thereby lose all respect for it. To introduce the pony to the wire and ensure effectiveness, lead him close to it on a long halter shank and let him graze up to the wire. Shortly, his curious nature will cause him to sniff it and then touch his lips to it. The mild shock will cause him to jump back in surprise. Then take him to all sides of the pasture so that he realizes that he is completely surrounded by this unusual and disconcerting device.

An electric wire, or electric fence as it is usually called, should be placed just high enough to touch the pony's chest; if placed too high he may be clever enough to scramble under it without touching. Conventional fences of wire or wood should be 4 feet high for ponies, and 6 inches more is desirable if larger horses are also to be confined.

A pasture is only as good as its gates. They must be sturdy, non-sagging, and at least 8 feet wide. A secure locking device which the pony cannot undo with his teeth is essential. It is difficult for the amateur carpenter to construct a lasting and serviceable gate; they are best purchased from an agricultural supply store.

It is not within the province of this book to discuss the methods of cultivating pasture, since soils and grasses vary widely in the different climatic areas of the country. State and Federal agricultural agencies are extremely cooperative and knowledgeable in giving advice when requested. Very probably you will find a county agent who will tell you whether fertilizer is needed (and, if so, what kind will best do the job), what grasses or combinations of grass need to be planted and how often, methods of weed control, and answer the many other questions which will come to mind. So check with the experts—your family's taxes pay their salaries and they are there to serve you without fee.

Unless the pasture is an extremely large one relative to the number of animals that will be grazing, it should not be used for a combination of ponies and cows, or ponies and sheep or goats. Sheep and goats crop the grass closer to the ground than a pony does and he will be shortchanged for food. There is also the remote hazard of the pony being gored by the horn of an irate cow.

The ideal pasture, then, is one with secure fencing, a windbreak, shade trees, provision for constant supply of water (if not a brook, then a large tub), with the right combination of grasses, properly fertilized soil, and reserved for ponies only. Since the ideal pasture is seldom found, one must compensate for the drawbacks of whatever is available with judgment and intelligence and an understanding of the pony's needs.

IV

FEEDING

Grass is the pony's natural food in the wild state, where he grazes almost continuously and takes relatively little exercise. Hay—dried and cured grass—is also a staple feed essential to the domesticated pony's diet. In addition to nutrition, hay provides needed roughage. If the pony is ridden or driven only occasionally, then grass or hay will suffice to maintain his condition. If, on the other hand, the pony is given hard work, he will require some grain for muscle and pep in addition to the normal ration of grass or hay. The cardinal rule to observe is that a pony should have sufficient food to maintain his normal weight. The true pony breeds require the least grain; ponies with a mixture of horse blood need more, and the horse breeds always require some grain to support good health.

Grass and hay are eaten slowly and digested rapidly. Grain, a more concentrated food, is eaten quickly and digested slowly; it should be fed frequently but in small amounts, since the pony's stomach is quite small in relation to his size. Grain has the added characteristic of swelling when wet, hence the pony should be watered before being fed grain (water passes directly and swiftly through the stomach to the kidneys). If the pony drinks too much water within an hour after feeding, the water will swell the grain in his stomach and a severe digestive disturbance will usually result. This is particularly uncomfortable—and sometimes even fatal—because ponies are unable to vomit or belch and cannot obtain relief from the effects of overfeeding.

Water kept in the stall at all times is the best way of preventing the pony from drinking too much at any given time. Of course, if he is brought in hot and thirsty from exercise, he must be cooled out and allowed small sips of water until he is dry and his thirst is quenched before being placed in his stall; otherwise he may develop colic, or even founder.

Grain is the seed of cereal plants. Oats, barley, and corn are the principal types suitable for equine feed. Grain must be fed to ponies if they are undergoing hard or fast work; it is essential to their health and vigor. Of the several suitable grains, oats are far and away the best feed, and the standard to which all the others are compared. Good oats should weigh more than forty pounds per bushel—a bit more than a pound per quart if bought whole, or up to a pound and a quarter if bought crushed. Ponies and horses relish crushed oats, but they must be newly crushed. The disadvantage of buying crushed or crimped oats is that the quality of the whole oat, before treatment, cannot be determined with certainty. A reliable dealer is important, one who values his reputation. Whole oats should be clean, crisp, free of dirt, and smell nicely.

Barley is satisfactory, but not nearly as good as oats. It is a heavy feed which will compact in the stomach if not mixed with oats, bran, or chopped hay. It should be crunched or ground, but not finely.

Corn is relished by ponies. It should be fed on the cob and be several months old. Since it is fat-producing and tends to heat the blood, it should be fed only during the cold months. It is a good substitute for oats during the winter if the pony is doing little or no work and is turned out much of the time. Incidentally, in the British Isles and certain other parts of the Commonwealth, what we know in the United States as corn is called maize, and oats are referred to as corn.

In recent years there has been a widespread increase in the use of concentrated feed in the form of pellets as a substitute for both hay and grain, as well as the development and acceptance of what is loosely termed "horse feed," "molasses feed," or "sweet feed," which is a mixture of grain, molasses, and other ingredients. These products are relatively inexpensive and convenient for the person taking care of the pony to use. The benefits to the pony may be something else again. Chemically, these products satisfy diet requirements, but they are not natural foods—at least not in natural form—and they do not provide sufficient roughage. Furthermore, the buyer cannot tell by inspection the quality of the feed used, as he can from examining oats, for example. The manufacturers of "horse feed" do not state the quality of the ingredients used, and, since the market is competitive, there is no reason to assume that they would mix top-quality oats with molasses. Many ponies, and horses, too, are fed completely on these products and seem to do quite well, but oats, grass, and good hay remain the staple feeds in the stables that try to give the best care.

Bran, although less nutritious than oats, has a mild laxative effect and is of great benefit in keeping the pony regular. If fed daily, mixed in the oats, it tends to relieve digestive disorders; substitute a pound of bran for a pound of oats in the daily ration. A pound per day is enough, so proportion the bran among the feedings rather than issuing it in one fell swoop. Caution: not more than one-fifth of the total oat/bran mix should be in bran; thus if the pony is not being fed at least five pounds of oats daily (which many ponies are not), the bran should not be fed with the oats and should instead be given once weekly as a mash. To make a bran mash, stir three pounds of bran into a pot of boiling water. Add three teaspoons of table salt. Cover with a heavy cloth (a burlap bag will do nicely) and allow to steam. When cool enough to eat, pour off the water and feed. Clean the feed bucket immediately after feeding.

Carrots and apples are welcome tidbits and appetite stimulators. They should be fed by hand, with fingers extended stiffly and touching each other to avoid being inadvertently nibbled. The offering should rest on the palm of the hand so the pony will pick it up with his lips. Carrots should be positioned so that the pony must break them with his teeth; a carrot swallowed whole may choke him. An apple (or a carrot) a day is sufficient, and it is a mistake to turn a pony out in an orchard where he can gorge himself and wind up with a severe case of colic.

Linseed meal makes the coat bloom—an old trick of a lazy groom. A little goes a long way; a tablespoon mixed in with the grain once a day will do the trick. Too much will cause disorder, so don't overdo it. And don't expect a miracle coat overnight—it takes time.

Never feed sugar to a pony. It is bad for the teeth and not necessary for health, since carbohydrates in the feed are converted to body sugar as needed. One all too often sees a misguided rider, wanting to reward his mount for a pleasant ride, offer a lump of sugar upon dismounting. While the intention is laudable, the practice can turn a well-mannered pony into a biter; having been taught to expect sugar at the end of a ride, he will start to bite in frustration if it is not forthcoming. Giving carrots or apples as a reward can also cause bad habits.

In addition to grass (or hay), and grain as needed, the two other essentials in a pony's diet are salt and water. Both should always be available, night and day, both in stable and at pasture. Salt is most easily handled in brick form rather than loose. In the Great Lakes area of the Midwest, iodized salt is necessary to make up for the lack of iodine in the soil. The simplest way to ensure that the pony is getting

all his needed minerals is to provide him with trace mineral salt bricks, of which there are several brands.

What and how much to feed are questions that can only be answered by trial and error, since they are affected by variables, including age, size, weight, breeding, and exercise. Study the effects of feeding and act accordingly, rather than by rote. No two ponies require exactly the same amounts. The figures in the table below are a range, the least amount indicating a ration (a ration is a day's supply) for an animal doing light work; the higher figure denotes the probable requirement to sustain hard or fast work, and the grain portion should be cut in half on idle days.

	Small Pony	Large Pony or Pony/Horse	Horse
Hay (lbs.)	8–10	10–12	12–20
Grain (lbs.): (select any one group)			
a. Oats	1–4	3–6	9–12
b. Oats } Bran }	—	3–5 / 1–1 / 4–6	7–10 / 2–2 / 9–12
c. "Molasses" or "Sweet" feed	1½–5	4–7	10–14
d. Oats } Corn }	½–3 / 1–1 / 1½–4	2–5 / 2–2 / 4–7	7–10 / 2½–3 / 9½–13
e. Oats } Barley }	1–3½ / 0–1½ / 1–5	3–5 / 1–2 / 4–7	6–9 / 4–5 / 10–13
Linseed meal (tablespoon)	1	1	2
Salt, trace mineral (brick), unlimited			
Water, fresh, unlimited			

As mentioned before, feed hay from the ground; feed grain from a tub in the diagonally opposite corner (of a box stall). Put the water bucket in a third corner.

Little mention so far has been made of hay except to emphasize its importance as a grass substitute. Unless the owner wants to go to the unwarranted expense of importing racetrack quality hay, or is fortunate enough to live in one of the few areas where really top-quality hay is locally grown, one must make do with whatever is available from nearby sources. Buy hay in bales from a reputable dealer, specifying at least a number two grade of the best local cutting. Upland meadow hay with a maximum of timothy, a small amount of clover, and a minimum of orchard grass is a very satisfactory mix. Look for greenness and plenty of leaf. Hay fed to cows is not of a quality suitable for ponies—always specify *horse* hay. Remember that hay provides much-needed bulk (in addition to nutrition) and resist the food store salesman's persuasive blandishments to buy hay pellets for convenience.

Certain general principles of feeding should always be observed, regardless of the amount fed:

Bear in mind that the grain ration is in *pounds*, not quarts. Mark the measuring device (a two-pound coffee can will do nicely) so that it can be filled to the proper level by weight. Check the weight of each hay bale (the dealer will have inserted a weight marker) and estimate the pounds to be given the pony by breaking the bale proportionately; for example, one-sixth of an eighty-pound bale will provide thirteen to fourteen pounds.

Feed regular amounts at regular intervals.

Issue one half the hay ration the last thing at night before going to bed. Distribute the other half proportionately during the day, prior to each graining.

Three feeds of grain per day are best if the total grain ration is more than four pounds. Always feed at least twice per day. Do not feed more than two pounds to a pony at any one feeding (or more than four pounds to a horse).

Never feed a full meal to a hot or tired pony. He should be cooled off and given a smaller than normal portion. Better yet, substitute a bran mash.

If the pony is being fed grain because he is being given hard work, reduce the grain ration by one-half on days when he will not be working.

Feed some hay before grain. Make sure thirst is quenched at this time, before the grain is fed.

Buy good quality hay and grain. Never give a pony moldy or dirty feed.

Feed according to the pony's condition, enough to maintain normal weight and provide the energy for the work he is asked to do, but avoid overfeeding. A fat pony, "feeling his oats," can be a handful of trouble.

V

EQUIPMENT AND TACK

Good quality stable equipment is an economy over the long haul because of the wear and tear it will withstand. Cheap equipment, on the other hand, will break or wear out at exasperating moments, must be more frequently replaced, and is never completely satisfactory. The difference in cost between cheap and good (not deluxe) equipment is slight, and well worth the additional investment. Even a casual scanning of a stable equipment catalog will reveal an impressive list of products for sale. A great many of these are gadgets to entice the novice or overenthusiastic pony owner, or else they are specialized items that seldom if ever will be needed for the typical backyard pony. The listing below of basic stable equipment is a rather comprehensive one to begin with; add to it only when the need becomes obvious.

Tack is a special classification of equipment which, by definition, means the accouterments which go on the pony—harness, saddle, bridle, halter, and related gear. As with the equipment used to care for the pony, it pays dividends to get good, serviceable tack and avoid the inferior qualities. The basic items of tack for a riding pony will vary somewhat by type, according to what bit he goes best in, the saddle best suited for the work he is asked to do, and other factors. However, the following list, which is intended for a pony that will be hacked and hunted, will be appropriate for most situations:

Saddle. Must be of a good fit, or back sores are sure to develop shortly. When viewed from behind, there should be air space all along the backbone. If the pony's withers are especially high or prominent, a "cut back" pommel is desirable to avoid rubbing. The saddle must also fit the rider, and one with the deepest part of the seat midway between pommel and cantle will not only prove most comfortable, but also help the rider to maintain the desired "balanced" seat. The *stirrup leathers* should be strong, flexible, and of good width. Twist new leathers so that they will allow the *stirrup irons* (which should be large enough so the foot fits easily into them) to hang at about an angle of 30 degrees; this makes it easy to find them with the toe without looking down when mounted. The girth should be of the three-buckle type. The Balding or Fitzwilliam patterns are constructed to minimize the possibility of creating girth sores. The string type has the advantages of being lightweight and nonchafe, but deteriorates more quickly than leather, loses strength in time, and is more trouble to keep clean.

Bridle. Should be of good quality and include a *cavesson,* or noseband. Although sewn-in reins and cheek straps are de rigueur in the hunting field and show ring, they are difficult to keep clean and soft in the loops. Best all-around construction is the stud fastening which permits opening for cleaning. Not recommended is the buckle construction (except to join the two ends of the snaffle rein); it catches on twigs, can rub or cut skin, and is generally unsightly.

Martingale. If the pony will go quietly at speed or over fences without tossing his head, there is little need for a martingale. On the other hand, a standing martingale is good protection against a rider's broken nose—it prevents the pony's poll from making contact. If worn, a standing martingale should be loose enough to allow normal head action; a restricted head can cause a fall, since the pony uses his head as a balancer. Running martingales are unsuited to short-necked ponies.

Halter. If of leather, should be of sufficient width to avoid cutting or rubbing the skin. A braided cotton "watering bridle" makes an ideal pony halter for use around stable and for pasture turnout. The nylon or dacron types are long-lasting but are apt to chafe the skin.

Pads. If the saddle fits properly and the pony's back is in good hard condition, there is no need for a saddle pad, assuming that the rider rides in balance. A pommel pad should never be necessary—its purpose is to relieve pressure on the withers caused by an improperly fitted saddle; the remedy is to use a proper saddle. A folded army-type blanket, or a mohair blanket such as those used by cowboys, is superior to the felt and synthetic saddle pads advertised in catalogs.

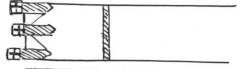

FITZWILLIAM 3-BUCKLE GIRTH

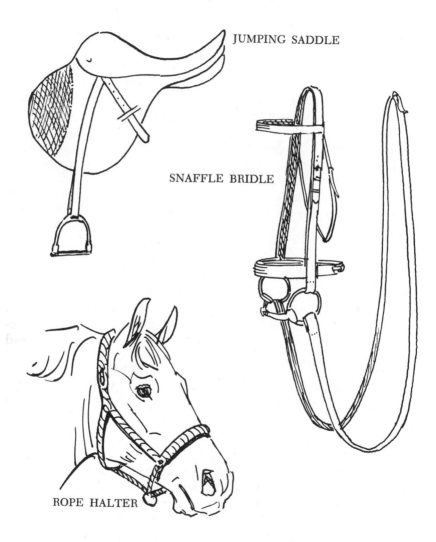

JUMPING SADDLE

SNAFFLE BRIDLE

ROPE HALTER

Grooming equipment should be cleaned frequently. If more than one pony is kept, each should have his own equipment kept in a small, individual box labeled with the pony's name; dandruff, lice, nits, dirt, and scurf are easily transferable by the indiscriminate use of grooming equipment. The pony's grooming box should include: three *sponges*—a large body sponge, and small muzzle and dock sponges (the rectangular, compressed type used for dishwashing are not suitable; use the loose-pored imitation of a natural sponge); four *combs*—a rubber currycomb for grooming the body, a metal curry-comb to be used only for cleaning out dandy and body brushes, a mane comb, and a tail comb; three *brushes*—a dandy brush, water brush, and body brush. *Rags* for rubbing down the coat can be made from discarded terry cloth bath towels or old linen dish towels.

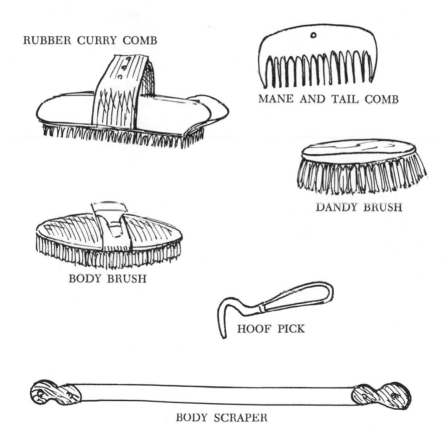

RUBBER CURRY COMB

MANE AND TAIL COMB

DANDY BRUSH

BODY BRUSH

HOOF PICK

BODY SCRAPER

A *hoof pick* and *scraper* are also needed, but one of each will do for all the ponies stabled. It is, however, a very good idea to have spare hoof picks available to be taken out riding.

Cleaning products for keeping leather and metal in good condition include: *saddle soap, neat's-foot oil, castile soap, glycerine soap,* a *leather preservative* such as Lexol, *sponges*—one for soaping the bridle and that part of the saddle coming in contact with the breeches, one for the underside of the saddle and the girth, and one for applying leather preservative. The sponges should not be interchanged and, of course, should never be used for grooming. Bits and brass are cleaned with *steel wool, metal polish,* and an impregnated *flannel cloth* such as Blitz. Old terry cloth toweling is good for drying and polishing metal and a *chamois* cloth can be very helpful for drying leather. A *saddle cleaning rack,* resembling a sawhorse, is a great convenience, as is a *bridle cleaning hook.* After cleaning, the saddle and bridle should be hung where air will circulate; a *saddle rack* and *bridle rack* can each be bought, or constructed at home. A 2′ × 4′ section, well sanded and braced and with the edges beveled, will suffice for the saddle rack, and an old saddle soap can (painted to prevent rust) nailed high on the wall, so the reins will hang without touching the floor, will make a perfectly satisfactory bridle rack. *Hooks* are convenient for crops, spurs, and hard hats. *Halter shanks* can hang from a nail as can the *twitch.*

BRIDLE RACK

SADDLE RACK

SADDLE CLEANING RACK

Close to the tack storage area should be a box containing *leg bandages, cotton wool,* a *shipping halter* (if a covered trailer is used to transport the pony). If the pony is to be clipped, his *blanket* and possibly a *cooler* should be hung on a long rod (the saddle blanket folds over the saddle when stored). One or two *water buckets* (not for drinking) are desirable aids—they have a hundred and one uses around a stable, including fire prevention, cleaning, and small article carrying.

A *first-aid kit* (for humans) can be considered optional, but desirable.

Tools should be kept in a secure area where the pony cannot step on them and injure himself. Stable tools that do not easily fit on a shelf should be hung on a wall, with holes drilled in the handle if necessary. They include: two *rakes*—one with bamboo prongs, the other the conventional iron-toothed model. Both should be as wide as possible. Two *forks,* one for hay and the other for manure (they are not interchangeable; manure will fall through a hay fork, for example). Two *brooms*—one the push type with stiff bristles such as one sees the sanitationmen use on city streets, and the other a household type. A flat-bottom *shovel* with curled sides, and a *manure basket.* Useful hand tools include: *hammer, pliers, wire cutter, screwdriver, leather punch,* and a sharp *knife.* An electrical outlet will permit the use of *clippers* and an *immersion heater* for making hot water. A *trash can* or large wastebasket should be kept handy.

The grain area must be kept secure from intrusion by a nocturnal pony, and may be combined with the tool area; since the grain area is likely to be somewhat dusty, tack should not be stored close by. A large stable, housing six or more ponies, is best served by feed bins for the grain; otherwise large galvanized trash cans with tight-fitting tops are recommended. The advantage of bins is that they are big enough to allow large quantities of feed to be ordered at a time. Buying in bulk saves time and usually costs less. The small stable is better off with the cans, since the grain will not become aged and moldy due to slow turnover. Two cans should be used for each type of grain. For example, if the pony is being fed oats and bran, there should be four cans in use. The purpose is to avoid the temptation to refill a partially empty can, leaving the older feed at the bottom. It is much easier to fill an empty can while the other is still an eighth or so full than it is to empty out the eighth and put it back on top. Two much smaller cans can be used for linseed meal. Large twenty-gallon cans are best for oats, "sweet molasses" feed, bran, and barley. Whenever a can is emptied, it should be thoroughly cleaned with hot water, scrubbed to remove all leftovers, and air dried—another advantage of the two-can-per-grain system. A lid latch is a good rat deterrent.

Finally, every stable should have a *fire extinguisher* and all persons using the stable should know how to operate it. If there is a water outlet nearby, a hose long enough to reach every part of the stable should be attached to the tap at all times.

VI

GROOMING AND SHOEING

Grooming, or the cleaning of a pony, improves his appearance and contributes greatly to the maintenance of health. Stabled ponies require more grooming than those on pasture. A pony kept in stable and worked under saddle or harness should have a thorough grooming daily, plus "backs and bellies" in the early morning and after work. Grooming does more than just keep the pony clean, desirable as that, of course, is; in the process of cleaning the pony, one will discover any injuries, sores, or heat and thus be able to nip infection or disease in the bud; furthermore, the massage effect aids muscle tone, stimulates circulation, and is a good conditioning agent.

Develop a systematic routine for grooming. In this way you will cover all the areas and miss nothing. The method developed by the U.S. Cavalry (which was vitally concerned with the care of horse-flesh, since a trooper's life might depend on his mount's condition) is a good one to follow, and is very similar to the one given below. First of all, tie the pony so that his head is comfortable but he cannot wander away from you. If possible, cross-tie him in an aisle where you have room to move around him. Then place the grooming kit box where he cannot step on it, take the rubber currycomb in your left hand, and approach the pony's near (left) side, ready to begin.

Work from front to rear, and from top to bottom. A good job will take from fifteen to twenty minutes, and it cannot be hurried. If you rush, you will only tire your arms, and not get through any sooner, so work slowly, carefully, and steadily, but put your back into it a bit.

Starting just behind the ears, rub the neck area with the rubber currycomb, using a circular motion and gradually working toward the shoulder. This will bring dandruff, dried dirt, and dead hair to the surface. Then take the dandy brush, also in the left hand (you brush and comb with the hand nearest the head), and go over the same area using short strokes with a flick of the wrist. The dandy brush should be applied in straight strokes, following the grain of the hair. Clean the rubber currycomb by rapping it against a wall, post, or your heel, and clean the dandy brush by passing the bristles across the teeth of the metal currycomb. Then, in order, repeat the comb and brush sequence on back, side, rump, and hindquarters, cleaning the equipment as needed. Next do the bottom line, starting between the forelegs and finishing up between the hind legs. Now check back and see if the poll (under the halter behind the ears), the base of the ears, and the entire belly area have been thoroughly groomed and cleaned; these are the areas most frequently neglected.

Now to the legs. The rubber curry may be used lightly between elbow and knee (the foreleg) and stifle and hock (hind leg), but it is not very effective over bone, and the dandy brush must do most of the work. Brush downward to the pasterns, paying special attenion to the back of the knee, front of the hock, and the creased skin where leg meets body. Clean the pasterns by brushing horizontally across them. The pony should be standing squarely on his foot when the pastern is brushed; if the pastern is bent—as it would be if it were to be picked up—the skin will be folded and proper cleaning will not be possible. Clean the comb and brush after doing each pastern and lay them aside while you take the hoof pick and clean out the soles of the feet. Never pull against the frog; always pick from heel to toe. Tap the side of the shoe on both sides to test for looseness. The trick in picking up a forefoot is to stand alongside the shoulder, lean down, and put a hand on the side of the hoof, lean a little weight against the shoulder, and lift as the pony shifts his weight to the other foreleg. To lift a hind leg, stand at the point of the hip facing the rear, lean down with the outside hand grasping the fetlock, and pull it toward you. As soon as the pony's leg starts to give, step forward with your inside leg and then bring your other leg forward. The pony's hind leg will then be pulled to the rear with his cannon resting across your inside thigh, and secured in place by your hand. It looks chancy but is completely safe—watch how the blacksmith does it.

The off (right) side of the pony is now groomed, following the same procedure used for the near side except that the currycomb and brush are operated with the right hand. Next comes the head, for which the dandy brush and rub rag are used. Gently stroke the dandy brush just in front of the ears to remove the marks left by the brow band of the bridle and use the rub rag for the rest of the head area. Always brush and rub with the grain of the hair.

Now for the mane (if any) and tail, each of which has its own metal comb. If tangled, start at the ends and gradually work to the base, then finish off with the dandy brush. There are no nerves in hair roots, so the application can be vigorous without hurting. If the mane has been particularly dirty, it may be the first order of grooming, so that the neck will not have to be done twice. If the mane or tail hair needs to be thinned, do a little each day, grasping bunches of two or three hairs at a time. When thinning the tail, start at the top and work down, making sure to take equal amounts of hair from each side. To train the mane to fall all on the same side, wet it and brush it, and then braid it and leave it alone except for occasional wetting down if it flops out of place.

The last essential is sponging the nostrils with clean cool water and the dock and sheath with lukewarm water. The sponges should not be interchanged; use three separate sponges and always use them only for the same area. Once a week the dock and sheath should be sponged with a soapy (not detergent) water, followed by a freshwater rinse. After sponging, the nostrils and lip area may be left wet, but both dock and sheath should be gently dried.

For a finishing touch, but not an essential one, complete the grooming by using the body brush over all the hair areas. Its soft bristles will not cause discomfort over the bony places and it will impart a sheen to the coat, as well as an extra massage for the patient pony. If time is short, this is the one phase of grooming that can safely be omitted.

"Back and belly" grooming is given after exercise and as an early-morning touchup. It consists of currycombing and dandy brushing the areas touched by saddle or harness, and bridle, as well as any obvious places where dirt is found. If the pony is hot after exercise, he must be cooled out before grooming. A convenient place to test for heat is to place a hand on the chest between the forelegs. If he is wet, but not hot, take the dandy brush and roughen up the hair to assist in drying. When dry, he is much easier to groom. The practice of washing down a pony is not beneficial, and may be harmful. Elbow grease is better than soap and water.

Ponies are best off without shoes if they are not required to travel hard roads and are not being given much work. Shoes are a necessary

WELL-SHOD HOOF   UNSHOD, UNEVEN HOOF

evil which must be tolerated to avoid undue wear and tear on the hooves. Ponies turned out at pasture do not need shoes and they should be removed and the hoof trimmed from time to time. The wall of a pony's hoof is like a fingernail; it can withstand a certain amount of friction but will break or crack under strain and it is in a constant state of growth. Because of growth, it must be trimmed regularly— every five or six weeks on the average—regardless of whether or not shoes are worn. A barefooted pony will wear some of the hoof down just in the normal course of his daily activity, but a shod pony's hoof will grow uninhibited, and the shoes must be removed and the hoof pared down.

A good blacksmith is worth his weight in gold, and just about as hard to find. The old-time craftsmen who believed in making the shoe fit the foot have been almost entirely replaced by incompetents who want to make the foot fit the shoe. The most abominable practice of these modern-day wonders is to heat the shoe and place it against the sole, thus burning the horn to fit the plane of the shoe. This treatment, the "hot potato" school of shoeing, will eventually dry out and rot the hoof. If you value your pony, make sure the blacksmith understands that the shoe is to fit the foot, and make sure that you are present while the shoeing job is being done. He should first trim the hoof and level it off so that the pony will move squarely. When the foot is level it should make an approximate 35-degree angle with the ground; if straighter, the pony will tend to "knuckle over" and his trot will be uncomfortable. If the angle is too great, the pony will be coon footed, and, although his gaits will be very comfortable for the rider, there will be undue strain on the tendons which could lead to a breakdown. After the foot is leveled, both the owner and blacksmith should look for injuries, and observe the pony's way of going; that is, how does he move at the walk and jog? He may be moving short, or interfering, or forging, or he may have a shrunken frog or quarter crack. All these defects, and others, may be alleviated by corrective shoeing, which is why a good blacksmith is worth his price. The smith then constructs each shoe to fit the pony and helps to correct any deficiencies of leg movement. He tailors each shoe to each foot and frequently tests a cool shoe against the prepared sole until a perfect match is made. When you find such a blacksmith, hold on to him come hell or high water. He may be a time-wasting, garrulous eccentric and a total bore, but he's your pony's best friend.

VII

MANNERS AND VICES

No pony is born vicious or ill-mannered; he becomes what man makes him and his faults are the result of man's cruelty, ignorance, and indifference. A pony reflects his master—assuming it has been a long-time association—and much can be learned about the human by observing the equine. True, some ponies are more high spirited than others, or more timid, or more intelligent; but these are differences of degree rather than of basic characteristics. Remember that the pony is a creature of habit and that his habits, once acquired, are extremely difficult to change.

Bad habits are termed *vices* if they take place in the stable, and *bad manners* if they occur under saddle or in harness. Their prevention begins as soon as the pony is foaled and exposed to humans. If he is a homebred, then the problem simply becomes one of intelligent handling and patient schooling. On the other hand, as most frequently happens, a pony may have gone through several owners before coming into your possession and his habits—for better or worse—may be very well established and deep rooted. Let us therefore discuss below the most common vices and bad manners and their causes and treatment. With patience and understanding some can be cured and others modified; a few, once acquired, are almost impossible to do much about.

VICES

Stable vices, as a group, are almost invariably the result of cruelty or neglect. They are habits learned as a defense against unthinking humans or as a result of boredom. As Erasmus said in 1515, "prevention is better than cure."

Cribbing, or gnawing the woodwork, is a nervous habit emanating from boredom. It cannot be cured, but may be completely prevented by covering the exposed wood edges of stall walls and other projections with metal. If this is impractical, a cribbing strap should be worn; this broad band of leather encircles the neck at the throat and is tightened so that the pony cannot distend the throttle muscles. A properly adjusted cribbing strap will permit eating and drinking, but it must be fitted carefully since too tight an adjustment will interfere with breathing. Both cribbing and wind sucking (see below) are encouraged by penning the pony in his stall for long periods of time; ponies kept in pasture or paddock except when absolutely necessary to bring them indoors are seldom prone to cribbing.

Wind sucking is akin to cribbing in cause and treatment, but is a far more serious vice in that it is debilitating to the pony's health. It is a nervous habit: the pony grasps the edge of a piece of wood or metal with his teeth, extends his head, tightens the throttle muscles (at the base of the throat), and grunts. The process of grunting may be an attempt to relieve gas on the stomach, but it is more probable that the grunt precedes an intake of air—a sucking in of wind. A cribbing strap is the only remedy.

CRIBBING

Weaving, another nervous habit fostered by boredom, makes it difficult to keep the pony in good condition. The pony will stand in his stall, head down with forelegs slightly askew, and shift from side to side for hours on end. The habit is contagious; isolate a weaver from the other stablemates or hang the open sections of the stall with burlap so that the offender cannot be seen by sound ponies. There is no known cure, but weavers seldom practice this habit in pasture; therefore prevention becomes a matter (as with cribbing and wind sucking) of giving the pony plenty of outdoor liberty. Box stalls are somewhat less conducive to developing the habit than straight stalls, possibly because they afford more freedom of movement. Also, some weavers will drop the habit if moved to an end stall where they can see activities going on inside and outside the stable.

Tail rubbing is normally a sign of lice in the hair or worms in the intestines. Correction of the cause will eliminate the practice.

Crowding in the stall is an attempt to avoid being handled, and usually is done in remembrance of rough treatment in the past. Take a broom handle or other stout stick and trim it to a length slightly longer than the width of your body. Enter the stall with stick in hand. As the pony starts to crowd you against the wall, place one end of the stick against the wall and let the pony bring his side against the other end. Meanwhile you are safely in the open space between wall and pony. Let the pony jab himself; he will quickly learn to respect the stick. As he learns that he will not be roughly handled (it takes a period of weeks to build his confidence), the stick will become unnecessary. Crowding is one of the few vices that can usually be completely cured.

Stall kicking is a habit of temperamental or high-strung horses at feeding time, and seldom found in ponies. Some pony mares will, however, kick the walls when in heat. A padded box stall, using old condemned cotton mattresses, will ease the damage to legs which can result. *Knee banging,* a similar habit, can be mitigated by keeping the pony in knee pads, leather devices with a foam lining which are held in place by straps. If the pony kicks or bangs out of impatience at feeding time, make every effort to feed promptly; if there are several ponies in the stable, feed the impatient one first.

Turning the rump toward a person entering the box stall is often a bluff to intimidate the rider or groom. It is caused by past mistreatment. If the pony is bluffing, as will soon be determined, a slap on the rump will turn him away. If he persists, then stern measures are in order to discourage and break the habit. Take a crop or halter shank in hand and open the stall door, speaking sharply to the pony. If he starts to present his rump, give it a solid, businesslike thwack with the crop or snap of the shank. Be alert for a retaliatory kick if the pony is greatly surprised. If you are consistent each time you enter the stall, the pony will soon learn that you mean to prevail, and give up his attempt to thwart you. Meanwhile encourage him to present his front, rather than his rear, by carrying a tidbit—a carrot or apple—with you and feeding it to him at the stall door; he will learn to anticipate your arrival and to wait in the desired attitude.

Pulling back. A few ponies kept in straight stalls develop the habit of backing out rapidly as soon as the tie is released. The remedy is to install a chain on the posts at the rear of the stall, adjusted to catch the pony just above the hocks. Then go to his head and untie him. The harder he hits the chain, the more meaningful the lesson. Take him up to the front of the stall and start backing him step by step; if he rushes, the chain will give him another lesson. If he steps back like a gentleman, discard the chain. Most ponies will learn to stand when untied in a stall after a very few lessons with the chain; some few will have to have the experience repeated from time to time.

Hard to bridle. A head-shy pony may have sensitive ears (which should be checked for fungus), or teeth which need to be floated (filed) to smooth out the rough edges made uncomfortable by the bit, or may just be playing with the short rider unable to reach his extended poll. If the reason is a physical one, the cause should be determined and treated; if the head tossing then persists out of habit, the bridle should be unbuckled at the near-side cheek piece, eased onto the head and over the ears, and rebuckled. The remedy for bridling a too-tall pony is to stand on a box.

Kicking in stable. Ponies learn to kick as a reaction to, and defense from, mistreatment. Kindness and patience, together with immediate punishment with a crop or halter shank when the offense occurs, will work wonders for all but the worst offenders. A pony that persists in kicking should be disposed of. The most docile pony may kick when greatly startled; always speak to him when approaching from the rear to let him know you are there—he may have been sleeping while standing up. The best protection against injury from a kick (apart from staying outside kicking range) is to stand close to the pony so that, if he should let fly, the contact will be more of a shove than a rapid blow. Also, a hand on the rump as you walk around him will allow you to feel if the pony is about to kick and give you time to get out of the way.

Charging and savaging. A pony madly galloping directly at a person walking through a field can be an unnerving experience, particularly if the four-legged whirlwind gives no indication of slowing down. Ponies that have been hand-fed as a means of catching them up in pasture are likely to acquire this bad habit of charging. In its extreme form it becomes coupled with nipping and, finally, biting (savaging).

The obvious solution is not to make too much of a pet out of the pony so that he does not become eager to rush up to a person at the pasture or paddock gate. For a pony that has the habit, it is best to carry a crop and whack him severely over the nose (it may take courage to stand fast as he approaches). Do not run; the pony will pursue and you will be at the disadvantage of having him behind your back and bearing down on you while you have no defense. Hitting his nose will break the habit, but it may not result in making him easy to catch in pasture; therefore do not spoil him to begin with. The one exception to standing fast and whacking the pony's nose is when the pony is a stallion with a band of brood mares. He will probably attempt to savage you despite punishment; give him a wide berth.

Hard to catch in pasture. Tidbits in the hand will entice the pony to come to you, but the disadvantage of this method is that it may develop into a habit of charging, as described above. Better strategy is to walk slowly behind him, gradually moving him into a fence corner where he may be picked up with ease. It is helpful to take advantage of the pony's habits and call for him at pasture when he knows it is time for feeding at the stable. You will probably find him waiting at the gate; all ponies have clocks in their heads when it comes to knowing mealtime.

BAD MANNERS

Bad manners are vices acquired as a result of poor training methods, usually when the pony has been repeatedly asked to perform something he does not understand, or when he has been allowed to get away with conduct for which he should have been punished.

Rearing, a defense against moving forward, is unwittingly taught by riders with heavy hands and poor legs. The alert rider will anticipate the bunching of muscles and going "behind the bit," which are preliminary to the rearing action, and compensate by sitting well forward and vigorously applying the spurs. It is a battle that must be won or the pony will soon start to rear whenever the spirit moves him. A weak rider should never be given a pony to ride that has a tendency to rear. The same pony, under a competent rider, will seldom attempt this defense. A confirmed rearer, especially one who will go all the way over backward, should not be used for a family pony.

Whirling is a similar defense to rearing in that the pony refuses to go forward and attempts to unseat the rider. The quick remedy is to encourage the whirling at a more rapid rate than that which the pony started, keep him circling with a bent spine for four or five tight revolutions and then push him with the legs in the wanted direction as he comes out of a turn. Whirlers, like most rearers, quickly become

PONY WHIRLING

discouraged when dominated and seldom attempt their tricks under riders who have proven their mastery.

Bolting, like so many other bad manners, takes advantage of weak riders. If the pony finds that he can take off for the stable as soon as he is turned around from the outward bound leg of the ride, he will be tempted to do so. A pull on the reins is useless, since the stronger pony will always win a tug-of-war against the rider. Half halts are an effective means of rating the eager pony; in severe cases he should be circled, turned sharply until he is somewhat dizzy. A *runaway* is, in effect, the same as bolting and is corrected by the same means. Runaway ponies usually are setting their jaws against a hard-handed rider, and the only ultimate solution is for the rider to develop good hands. All riders should learn how to apply the pulley rein, a severe method of stopping a bolter or runaway in midflight and therefore to be applied only in emergency.

Shying has many causes, but essentially is a reaction to unexpected sounds or unfamiliar sights. Bear in mind that a pony's eyesight is unlike man's; he sees in various shades of gray and is quite near-sighted. A large boulder may resemble, in his mind's eye, a bear; a steamroller working on the road can be a terrifying object which he is unable to comprehend. There is no way that shying at loud noises, such as thunder or thoughtless tooting of an automobile horn, can be prevented; the rider must simply soothe the pony by voice and neck-patting while at the same time using the legs to induce forward movement. Nervousness at approaching unfamiliar objects can usually be anticipated as the pony shows signs of alarm and hesitancy. Let him look carefully at the object, speak in a soothing voice, and use the legs judiciously to make him maintain the wanted gait and direction. Familiarity breeds contempt—once the pony realizes that the object means him no harm he will ignore it the next time it is met, provided the rider has been understanding yet firm. In severe cases the pony may whirl away from the object; the cure for this is to treat it as a whirl (see above) and dominate the situation. Never let a pony win a shying contest, else he will feel free to shy at will. As with so many instances of bad manners under saddle, a rider's weak legs will encourage disobedience and strong legs will discourage the

attempt. The use of a crop as a replacement for weak legs is a poor substitute; however, if one does carry a crop, the pony will know it is there and the psychological effect can be helpful.

Refusing to jump can be considered to be bad manners only when the approach has been good and the object not too difficult for the pony's ability. In such instances the cause is almost always the fault of the rider's heavy hands or weak legs. All ponies, sooner or later, will refuse if they are not certain that the rider really means to jump (the "spurring forward and pulling back" syndrome). When a pony has refused out of willfulness—rather than from a bad approach or an inept rider—he should be immediately punished; present his chest to the jump, restrain forward movement by tightening the reins, and attack his sides with the spur. Then take him back ten or fifteen yards, face the jump, gather the pony, and put him once again to the task, using the leg vigorously. Not to do so will quickly develop a treacherous and unsafe animal. It should be remembered that the pony will not jump a fence in nature; it is only to please man that he assays this gymnastic.

VIII

CONDITION

A pony in *good* condition is well muscled, not overweight, and has a bright coat. If he is too fat, the result of overfeeding and under-exercising, he is said to be in *soft* condition. If he has been given a period of hard training for hunting, horse show jumping, trail riding, or the like, he will be in *hard* condition if the combination of feed, exercise and work has been intelligently coordinated. Lastly, if he is listless, skinny, and dull-coated from improper care, he is in *poor* condition. Ponies should be kept in good condition at all times except when hard condition is desired. Soft and poor conditions are unfavorable reflections on the caretaker.

Most of the time it is sufficient to maintain the pony in good condition, with a bright coat, clear eye, a bit of a bounce early on a cold morning, a good appetite, an alert expression, and the indefinable quality of appearing to be glad to be alive. Regular exercise is an essential ingredient, and the amount of feed must be carefully watched to supply the necessary energy; too little will weaken him and cause a weight loss, whereas too much will soften him. It is difficult to maintain good condition with less than an hour and a half exercise daily (with one day off for rest on half rations). There is a difference in result between a casual ride and a period of work. You can take the pony out on a loose rein and take your own pace on a pleasure ride where he loafs along and gets little benefit, or you can ride him on contact, with active leg, and get much better results. Although the time spent in the saddle may be the same, the benefits to both mount and rider in terms of exercise are minimal on loose rein riding. Every ride should include a period of schooling; even on a country road one can practice "three speeds at the trot," shoulder in, the extended walk, and many other fitness exercises, all of which build suppleness, response, and muscle. The old French adage that "one should ride as much with the legs as with the hands" will ensure that the pony's gymnastic training, and hence his fitness, is not neglected.

Since no two ponies are exactly alike in their requirements for feed and exercise to maintain good condition, it is necessary for the owner to develop an "eye" that will tell him or her what adjustments are needed. Since the exercise program is usually determined by the time available, most adjustments are made by carefully apportioning the amount of feed in the daily ration. Start with the amounts discussed in Chapter IV, "Feeding," and vary slowly according to whether the pony gains or loses weight after he has reached the desired plateau of weight and muscle. If he starts off in fat condition, less feed is indicated at first. On the other hand, if he is in poor condition he must be somewhat overfed for a time. All changes in amount of feed should be made gradually, as should the amount of exercise. A fat pony cannot be worked too hard without risking respiratory and muscular damage; a pony in poor condition must be fed up before

POOR CONDITION

being given anything but a minimum exercise program; otherwise he may incur structural damage. Make haste slowly.

Good grooming is essential to maintain good condition. In addition to keeping the pony clean, the brush acts as a skin conditioner and massage device. A thorough daily grooming should be given, plus "backs and bellies" after exercise. Docks and sheaths should be sponged, hooves cleaned out, and mane and tail hair combed.

Ponies turned out to pasture can be brought back more quickly to good condition if fed a handful or so of mixed grain and corn daily, and provided with ample salt. If the pasture grass has insufficient nourishment, good hay should be fed as a supplement to grazing. In most areas of the country, grass starts to lose its value in midsummer. Ponies that have been on pasture are sure to have worms, and the feces should be periodically examined for this debilitating annoyance. It is good practice to worm any pony twice yearly, in early spring and mid-fall after the first killing frost; the veterinarian should be consulted first. Worming will cause a temporary setback in condition and therefore should not be employed within about two weeks of hunting, competitive trail riding, or other strenuous work.

To bring a pony into good condition—hardened into shape for hunting, for example—may take as much as six weeks if he has been long on pasture and has grown a "hay belly." First of all, he should be properly shod. Very probaby his back skin is soft and will be sensitive to the saddle. Brine is an excellent skin hardener (prizefighters use it on their fists) and may be lightly sponged around and behind the withers, then absorbed into the skin with the aid of vigorous hand slapping of the area. Two applications a day should be continued until the skin is so toughened that a blanket or pad is not needed for protection. Slow work is the key to obtaining good condition. The pony should be given all work at the walk for the first week or ten days, but on the bit rather than on a loose rein. When the belly has noticeably begun to harden, and the lathery sweat that typifies extreme softness has disappeared, the pony will then be ready for a combination of walk and trot, increasing the time of trotting gradually for the next two weeks. Cantering or galloping are necessary only to build wind; they will not keep a pony fit and can be harmful if overdone. It is entirely possible and practical to develop a pony into good, fit condition merely by slow work at the walk and trot, without any work at the canter or gallop. If the pony is to be given work at these faster gaits before he is in hard condition, it is important to watch his breathing with great care so that he does not overdo his respiratory capacity. Better to have him fit in all respects before taking up any cantering or galloping.

(58)

When time is a factor, or if for some reason the pony cannot be ridden for a while, the longe is an excellent means of giving him work. As with everything else connected with ponies, there is a right way and a wrong way to longe. Little benefit is derived if the pony is allowed to go round and round unbalanced; he must be kept collected and worked both ways (clockwise and counterclockwise) if the exercise is to be useful.

IX

FIRST AID AND DISEASE PREVENTION

First aid is defined as what to do in case of accident before the veterinarian comes. Always call for specialized help if there is heat or fever, and whenever you are not absolutely certain of being completely qualified and able to cope with the situation, no matter how slight the injury may appear to be.

Among the most common injuries to which a pony is prone are wounds, which are of four types: punctures, abrasions, incisions, and lacerations. All wounds are potentially dangerous because of loss of blood and the very real probability of infection.

Punctures are caused by a sharp instrument such as a nail or hay fork. Do not cover the wound, keep it open and clean away any dirt, using hot water and a clean rag.

Abrasions are caused by rubbing. A rubbed tailbone (usually caused by shipping without a tail bandage) may be smeared with Vaseline. Saddle and girth sores respond to a painting with methylene blue, repeated several times daily. The tack should be cleaned, and padded or otherwise altered to prevent rubbing in future. The pony cannot be used until the sore is entirely healed.

Incisions are cuts, as from barbed wire or shards of glass. The deeper they are, the more dangerous. Keep clean and paint with tincture of iodine; call the veterinarian if there is any possibility that the wound will require stitching, or if severe or prolonged bleeding occurs.

Lacerations are wounds in which the flesh is torn. If slight, paint with methylene blue and sprinkle some sulfa powder. Most lacerations require stitching, are prone to infection, and heal very slowly.

A *rope burn* is a special case of abrasion, usually occurring on a pastern or other flexible joint. If it should not respond to methylene blue, apply a thick coating of resinol ointment. The objective is to heal the wound without growing a scab.

Arterial wounds are recognizable by the spurting blood. Quick action is required. In those few areas where a tourniquet can be applied, as on a leg, apply it tightly above the wound. Release every fifteen minutes to avoid gangrene. If a tourniquet cannot be used, the only alternative is to apply pressure between the wound and the heart, experimenting to find a place that best reduces the flow. A wounded vein will flow, rather than spurt, and the pressure point is on the other side, that is, away from the heart. A tourniquet should not be used and the danger is much less than that of an arterial injury. Most wounds merely injure a few capillaries, which ooze for a while; cold compresses will hasten the stoppage.

Do not cover a bleeding wound; keep it open and let the flow act to wash away germs. Infection only begins when the blood flow ceases. Most wounds will tend to become infectious if given the slightest opportunity. Early symptoms are excessive heat, swelling, and soreness, followed a few days later by discharge of pus.

Fistula is a boil on the withers caused by an ill-fitting saddle. *Poll evil* is a similar boil formed on the poll, usually as a result of striking an object such as a branch or low beam, or being struck with a hard instrument. The early symptoms are as for newly healing wounds:

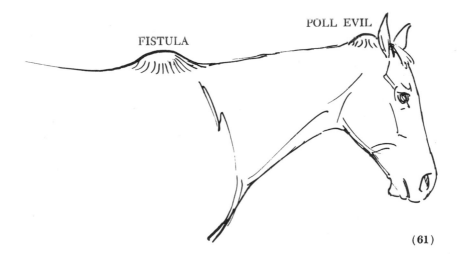

FISTULA

POLL EVIL

heat, swelling, and soreness. Early detection and treatment are vital lest you wind up with a pony that cannot be saddled or bridled.

The discharge of pus is a sign of a healing wound or boil, and should be encouraged once it has begun. Since the exuded material is concentrated infection, cleanliness and disinfection are paramount. Wear rubber gloves, coat the surrounding area with Vaseline (after first making sure it is clean and sterile) and bathe the exuding section with Lysol or some other antiseptic. Sulphatiazole should be applied as a healing agent. Make sure no traces of pus remain on the pony or the equipment used in treatment. Absorbent cotton, which can be disposed of, is best used to swab the area, and for applying the antiseptic.

Lameness has many causes, including overwork, bad shoeing, strains and bruises, thrush, infection or an infected wound, laminitis (founder), bowed tendons, hock weakness, and shoe boil among others. A lame pony should not be worked under saddle under any circumstances. Elderly ponies sometimes are a little stiff after a night penned up in their stalls or other confined areas such as a trailer. This is not necessarily lameness in the true medical sense; give the pony four or five minutes slow walk at the end of a lead line to see if he will work out of the stiffness and move normally.

Unless the source of lameness is apparent (which it usually is not), it can be found by trotting the pony on hard level ground, leading him on a loose shank so that his head movement is not restricted. A lame pony's head will nod perceptibly; he raises his head to take the weight off the injured leg. This method isolates the diagonal in which one leg (or shoulder) is sore; thus, assuming the pony raises his head as the left forefoot strikes the ground, the problem is in the left foreleg or right hindleg. Four times out of five it will be the foreleg. If he is then turned sharply, the affected leg will usually be obvious. If there is still a question, back the pony over a log or rail. Reluctance to back indicates the seat of the problem is in the shoulder rather than the leg. Now begins the minute examination to determine the exact nature of the lameness; a systematic procedure, such as the one suggested here, should be followed. Clean out the foot and tap the sole wih the flat of the hoof pick. Flinching indicates soreness—either a stone bruise, puncture wound, or corn. Smell the foot for thrush, which affects the frog, has a foul odor, and is usually accompanied by a watery discharge. Feel the wall of the hoof for heat, which would indicate laminitis or gravel working its way up the inside of the wall. Note: in feeling for heat one should simultaneously feel the corresponding section of another leg at the same time in order to make a comparison; in the case of laminitis, it is probable that both forefeet will be equally hot; therefore make the comparison with a hind foot.

Assuming the foot passes inspection, move to the leg and test for heat, tenderness, and swelling. Start at the elbow or stifle and work slowly down to the coronet. Should this examination not prove fruitful, the cause is most likely in the shoulder (if the foreleg does not move naturally) or the stifle (if the problem is with the hind leg). Lift and bend the leg to find if the pony resists movement; he will be particularly resistant to a high leg lift if the problem is in the stifle. A lame shoulder is often indicated by the pony's reluctance to put his foot flat on the ground—he prefers to rest on the front tip of the foot. The final point of examination in the case of hind-leg lameness is in the hip area. A dropped hip is easily noticeable by standing behind the pony and observing that it is lower than the sound opposite hip, the usual cause being a severe contact with a post, door frame, or stall corner. Assuming the hip appears normal, the area should then be pinched and pressed; if the pony flinches, the muscle is sore.

When examining the hind legs, look for aberrations in the hock region, either a curb, a cap, a thoroughpin, or spavin. Ringbone, sidebone, and splints are normally found only on the forelegs.

Washes, mild blisters, bandaging, and other treatments may help alleviate some causes of lameness, but nothing takes the place of complete rest in which the pony is turned out to pasture or paddock with shoes removed. This writer strongly believes that pin firing, which is an extremely painful form of torture, should never be used (see glossary); the only benefit is to render the pony unfit for work for a long period of time and thus enforce a rest.

Some of the more common forms of lameness and their treatment are:

Shoe boil (capped elbow) is formed on the point of the elbow, usually caused by the pony sleeping with his forefoot bent under him in such a position that the shoe rubs the elbow. Although unsightly, a shoe boil will only cause lameness if it grows to such an extent that it interferes with free movement of the leg. The condition is treated as a boil, extracting the pus when the boil comes to a head. Prevention involves equipping the pony with a special boot while stabled, plus corrective shoeing.

A *splint* is a bony growth on the side of the cannon bone, known as a high splint if close to the knee or a low splint if part way down the leg. High splints frequently cause lameness in young ponies and are the result of working them too hard over hard surfaces. Rest and slower work are the best treatment, in combination with a mild blister.

A *ringbone* is a circular bony growth between the fetlock and the coronet. A *sidebone* occurs when the lateral cartilage of the foot ossifies, or turns to bone. Although quite common in workhorses, they are seldom found in ponies unless they have been given prolonged

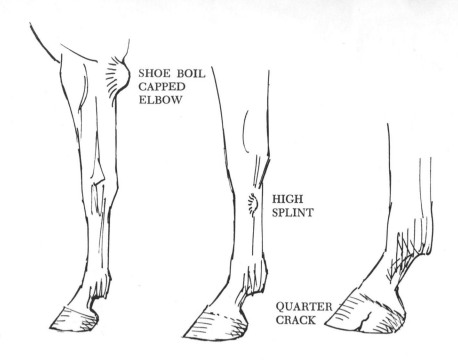

SHOE BOIL
CAPPED
ELBOW

HIGH
SPLINT

QUARTER
CRACK

periods of trotting on hard-paved roads. There is no cure, but, except in very advanced cases, the pony may be ridden normally as long as he is not asked to trot on hard ground or jump demanding fences where the landing would cause undue impact.

Quarter crack is a split-hoof condition caused either by the feet having been kept too dry for a protracted period of time or by the blacksmith having cut away too much of the heel when fitting the shoe. The condition is seldom found in ponies that work on soft ground. Since the hoof wall grows slowly—at the rate of about one-third of an inch per month—the shoes should be removed and the pony turned out to pasture or paddock as soon as a crack is observed. Quarter cracks are painful and cause the pony to go severely lame if worked. In some instances the condition is aggravated by a weak or brittle hoof. Gelatin powder added to the feed will provide some strengthening to a weak hoof just as it does with the human fingernail. The hoof must grow out, being trimmed carefully in the meanwhile, in order to eliminate the crack.

Corns are located in the heel, just under the shoe. A corn is a bruise on a very sensitive part of the foot and pressure upon it produces lameness. The remedy is corrective shoeing so that the shoe will bear no weight over the corn, which will then gradually heal itself. The veterinarian should decide whether or not to cut the corn out.

Laminitis (founder) is a most painful inflammation of the blood vessels of the feet. It usually results from overworking the pony and allowing him to drink quantities of water without further exercise. The symptoms are obvious even to the untutored eye: severe lameness and, if the pony can be induced to walk, he will move as if walking on eggs. Excessive heat will be found in the entire foot. Shoes must be removed with great gentleness and the pony stood in running water or, better yet, deep mud, for many hours. A pony that has been foundered will develop ribbed rings around the hoof wall—a permanent indicator of the permanent injury he has suffered. In mild cases the pony may eventually be used again, but only for the lightest type of work. Laminitis, when it occurs, usually affects both forefeet.

Scratches are similar to chapped hands in humans and are caused by cold, wet mud in the springtime. They are found in the pasterns just above the heel. Prevention simply involves thoroughly cleaning and drying the backs of the pasterns during grooming. Treatment requires that the pony be kept off muddy ground and that the affected area be soaked with a warm solution of boric acid or Lysol. Scabs and crusts should be soaked off and the underpart covered thickly with a bismuth base powder.

A *dislocated stifle* calls for prompt veterinarian attention. The amateur should not attempt treatment, other than to keep the pony on his feet until help arrives.

Thrush is an infection of the frog of the foot, often the result of failure to keep the stall floor clean of manure and urine, in combination with lack of cleaning out the feet during grooming. Thrush, therefore, is a severe reflection on the groom's ability to take proper care of his or her pony. Aggravated cases of thrush cause lameness. Copper sulfate, crushed finely and worked well into the frog, is a good remedy. The sole must then be packed with cotton to retain the medicament, which is replaced daily.

A *thoroughpin* is a swelling between the tendon and the bone just above the hock. Soft and "doughy" to the touch, it is a blemish rather than an unsoundness, but it is an indication of overwork and weakness in the hock joint. Similarly a *bog spavin*, which appears on the inner front side of the hock, is unsightly, indicates a weakness, but is not an unsoundness. In contrast, a *bone spavin* (or "jack") is a serious matter which eventually will cause permanent stiffness. It is a bony growth on the inner side of the hock for which there is no cure.

A *curb* is a swelling directly below the point of the hock, and is a symptom of a ruptured tendon. In slight cases apply iodine or some other mild blistering agent once daily for three days and then stop the treatment for another three days, repeating the cycle if necessary. If the pony is not lame, he may be given light work. If the curb is pronounced, a heavy blister and complete rest are needed.

(65)

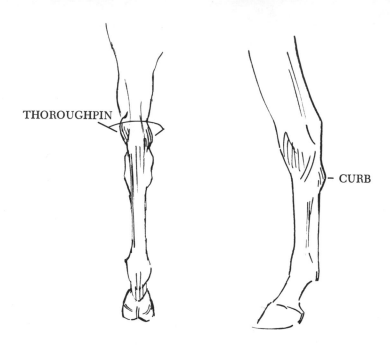

THOROUGHPIN

CURB

Capped hocks are the result of injury, usually from kicking the stall wall. If the habit persists, either pad the wall with old cotton mattresses or transfer the pony to a standing stall. The treatment is as for a curb.

A *bowed tendon* is a serious breakdown directly behind the cannon bone and is most common in animals that have been worked at extreme speed. The tendon becomes permanently enlarged and the pony is usually very lame. Strong blistering is indicated, with shoes pulled and the pony turned out to pasture for a prolonged rest.

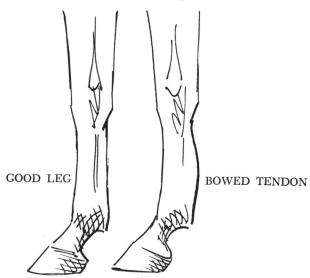

GOOD LEG

BOWED TENDON

In addition to the injuries and wounds that are caused by overwork, neglect, and accident, it is important to recognize some of the serious respiratory, digestive, and other ailments to which equines, particularly those kept in stable, are susceptible.

Coughs result from overwork, overexposure, and bad feeding. They are highly contagious; isolate the coughing pony from his mates and make sure that he does not share a common watering pail or trough. The pony should be kept warm with a blanket and away from drafts. A hot bran mash is helpful and should be given daily. However, a coughing pony will have little appetite for any food and may reject the mash at first until he becomes really hungry, so persist. Call the veterinarian and ask him to prescribe medication. *Shipping fever,* similar to a cough in symptoms and cause, can be distinguished by an accompanying nasal drip. If not caught in time, it may develop into *strangles,* with excessive nasal discharge and swelling of the throat and jaw glands. Strangles require the services of a veterinarian.

Heaves (asthma) is an incurable respiratory ailment. The pony exhibits a hacking cough, has difficulty in breathing, and shortness of wind. The flanks will heave (hence the name) after mild exertion. Exposure to dust must be minimized, since dusty hay, combined with overwork, is the principal cause of the condition. The ailment may be alleviated, but never cured, by avoiding dusty trails and paddocks, wetting down the grain and hay, using a veterinarian-prescribed cough medicine, and avoiding prolonged exertion. Special commercial feeds are available and seem to be effective in some instances. When pony develops heaves, he must be immediately rested. To continue working him may be fatal.

Inflammation of the eye can be caused by dust, either from old hay (especially if fed from a rack or net rather than from the ground) or from a dust-stirred road. It is most common where ragweed grows. Bathe the watering eye with a warm solution of boric acid.

Colic, or acute indigestion, calls for immediate veterinary treatment and energetic action on the part of the pony's owner or groom until the veterinarian arrives. Do not delay; colic is the cause of a great many deaths. The cause is excessive feeding, eating wet grass, or excessive watering too soon after a meal of grain. Since the pony is unable to vomit, he generates gas internally which is difficult to expel. He will appear extremely uncomfortable, repeatedly getting up and down and biting and kicking at his side as the pressure mounts. While waiting for help keep him covered with a blanket, on his feet, and moving around at a walk. Rub the loins with liniment and give an enema of soapy warm water. A heart stimulant, nox vomica, will be helpful; give one teaspoonful on the tongue and do not repeat the dosage.

Kidney inflammation is caused by a blow or excessive weight on the small of the back. Exposure to cold may also cause the affliction. The pony will flinch while being groomed, or when the rider leans back in the saddle. He may flinch while being mounted. He will tend to stretch when standing, and move in a straddling fashion. Consult the veterinarian by phone; he will probably prescribe a tablespoonful of sweet spirits of niter in a mixture of water. Keep the pony blanketed and do not work him until the pain, as indicated by flinching, has gone.

Azoturia (Monday morning disease) is the result of overfeeding a pony in good condition without working him on the same day. The prevention is to cut the feed ration in half on days when he will not be used. The pony with azoturia loses control of his hindquarters, the muscles in the loin harden and go into spasm, and the temperature rises. He should promptly be blanketed and the loins covered with hot blankets. A hot enema should be given while waiting for the veterinarian.

A pony in good health stands firmly on his forefeet, the eyes are open, bright, and alert, and the ears appear to be strong and active. He has an air of alertness. The coat will have a gleam, the skin will be loose, and the breathing will be regular—about fifteen exhalations per minute. The pulse rate is thirty-six to forty per minute. The temperature range will be within a half degree of 100 degrees. Bowel movements occur about eight times daily with the droppings being just soft enough to split as they fall, but not slimy. The urine will appear somewhat thick and will be a light yellow color. There will be no heat in any of the limbs or feet. Once one learns to recognize the signs of a healthy pony, it becomes second nature to identify indications of a falling off in condition and then to isolate the problem.

Every home stable should have a medicine chest for the pony, including but not limited to:

Alcohol, rubbing
Bandages, gauze
Bandages, leg
Blue stone (copper sulfate)
Boric acid powder
Colic medicine (as prescribed)
Cotton, absorbent
Cotton pads
Enema bag
Gloves, rubber
Hoof, dressing

Iodine, tincture of (strong)
Liniment
Lysol disinfectant
Methylene blue
Safety pins
Scissors (blunt-ended)
Sulphathiazole
Thermometer, rectal
Vaseline
Worm medicine (as prescribed)

X

TRAILERING

Today's modern high-speed turnpikes and interstate Federal highways make it possible to take the pony far afield to horse shows, gymkhanas (meets featuring games and novelty contests), hunt meets, endurance rides, and vacation areas. A trailer hitched to the family car is the best way to transport the pony. There are a variety of trailers on the market to suit most pocketbooks, or one can be built at home by a handy carpenter. Any standard passenger car or station wagon can pull a one-horse trailer, but a medium or heavy vehicle is needed for a two-animal conveyance. State laws vary considerably, and thus cannot be treated in detail here. Whether required by law or not, a safety chain should always be used so that the trailer and car will not part company if the hitch should fail. The hitch should never be fastened to the car bumper; it should be welded to the frame of the car. The ball must be behind the bumper. Although not a legal requirement, the trailer should have a built-in jack and wheel at the front end as an aid to easy hitching; otherwise it will take considerable muscular effort to lift the trailer and set the socket on the ball.

If your pony is actually a small horse, the dimensions should be carefully checked before purchase of a trailer. A single-horse trailer should measure between thirty and thirty-two inches in width; anything more is dangerous, anything less will be confining. Similarly a

two-horse trailer should measure fifty-eight inches in width, or two more if a centerboard divider is installed. Length should be at least seven and a half feet, but eight is preferable; this measure refers to the stall space and does not include the forward area, which should add at least two more feet in length. All of these dimensions are *inside* measurements, so allow for roof and sidewall thickness when measuring. Of course, if you are trailering a small pony, these figures may be reduced somewhat. However you never know when you may want to trade up to a larger pony, or load a full-sized horse to accompany your own small pony, so it makes sense to have a trailer that can handle the big ones as well. There is not much of a market for a secondhand small-pony trailer.

In selecting a trailer there are certain features, in addition to size, that are desirable; conversely, there are some features of well-known makes that are highly undesirable and should be avoided:

Lights. Stop- and taillights are required in most states, and should be in all. Running lights are an added safety factor, as are reflectors. Although not very pretty to look at, large reflective lettering on the tailgate is an effective warning to tailgaters:

HORSES
KEEP BACK

Wheels. A two-wheel (one-axle) trailer is somewhat less expensive than a four-wheeler (two axles), but the difference is well worthwhile. A two-wheeler will rise in front as the pulling vehicle (the car) accelerates, thus tending to take weight off the car's rear wheels and disturbing its equilibrium. Similarly, the reverse action of slowing down places an overload on the rear end of the car and induces whipping or swaying. The pony travels very uncomfortably during all this seesaw action. A blowout of one tire on a single-axle trailer can capsize the load and cause a bad wreck, to say nothing of serious injury to the pony. Anyone who has had the experience of trying to unload large animals from an over-turned trailer will testify that it is an ordeal he is in no hurry to repeat. A double-axle, four-wheel trailer is far superior in terms of balance, stability, and tire safety than the single-axle two-wheeler. The best two-axle models have one set of wheels placed behind the center of balance and the other set placed an equal distance in front, the area between them extending approximately under the middle third of the trailer.

Tailgate construction should be solid. A rod and strap hinge—in effect a "king-sized" reinforced piano hinge—should run the full width of the trailer. Cleats are desirable to prevent slipping. A stout, tubing-covered, well-secured tail chain should be inset six inches in front of the tailgate, and positioned just above hock height.

A *full top*, rather than a front hood, is preferable, provided it allows enough headroom for easy loading. Not only does it make for sturdier construction of the trailer, it also provides much needed shelter from the elements. With a fully enclosed trailer, one can be sure that the occupants are comfortable and protected during inclement weather.

An *exit door* at the front is a great convenience to the loader and almost a necessity if the pony is at all fractious during loading or unloading. It can be dangerous to try to wriggle from his head to the exit ramp, or to attempt to enter from the rear in an emergency.

A two-animal trailer should have a divider in the center. It makes for easier loading if this is in the form of a movable bar, hinged at the forward end. When shipping a single pony in a two-pony trailer, the bar should be in place so that he will not stand sideways, or slip and fall. (Hint: when only one animal is the occupant of a two-animal trailer, place him on the left side. He will travel more smoothly when you leave the concrete highways and take the blacktop or dirt roads of the countryside, all of which are of "crowned" or side-sloping construction.)

A front unloading door is unnecessary, since the pony will unload much more easily than he will enter the trailer. The chest bar, or manger, should be extremely sturdy and set high enough to allow the pony to brace his chest against it in case of a sudden stop. If the manger is a partition reaching the floor, it should be padded (an old cotton mattress will do nicely) to prevent knee injury. The padding should clear the floor by at least six inches, otherwise it will be cut by shoes and contaminated with bedding and manure. The divider in a two-horse trailer should, as noted, be hinged at the front end and secured at the rear end so that it will resist the weight that is sure to be leaned against it from time to time. A full board, reaching the floor and shoulder high, will prevent a kicker from injuring his traveling companion, but a single bar allows more foot room, is easier to handle, and will do for all but fractious or extremely nervous animals. Chains and heavy snaps should be used to secure the halter to the trailer; the standard halter shank is too weak, particularly the cast-iron snap. Give the pony as much slack as possible, adjusting the chain length so that he can have maximum freedom of head movement without being able to bite the neck of another animal alongside. Remember that the head is his "balancer"; he will arrive in much fresher condition at the end of the ride if his head has not been cramped.

The tail chain, which should be covered with rubber tubing (an old bicycle tire serves admirably), is often used to secure the center divider. Its fastenings must be extremely sturdy and its position must be so located that the pony cannot get under it if he should back suddenly. Too high a location will cause tail rub, too low will injure hocks. The correct position is from six to eight inches below the prominent point of the buttocks. The installation of a tail chain is recommended, regardless of the method of fastening the centerboard divider, and should be installed at least six inches in front of the closed tailgate. It has two advantages: the pony is restrained from attempting to unload as soon as the tailgate is lowered, and it prevents the pony from leaning against the tailgate or kicking it while in transit.

Protective equipment should always be utilized, even when traveling a very few miles. If the headroom appears to be at all inadequate, a shipping halter should be used. This is essentially a halter with a pad inserted to protect the poll and can easily be made at home by altering a standard halter. Felt shipping boots, particularly on the hind legs, prevent damage to the coronary band from shoe calks as the pony shifts his legs to maintain balance. The two-section boot, with the upper section conforming to the lower leg and the bottom section covering the pastern and hoof, is best. A tail bandage will protect the hair and bone from rubbing If the trip is to be a long one, the forelegs—whether or not a shipping bandage is used—should be wrapped with support bandages.

Some ponies are very difficult to load, and the fault is almost invariably the result of bad handling or a frightening experience. With a green pony, who has never traveled in a small trailer, a little patience will go a long way. Loading is an element of horsemanship, just as are teaching the pony to back, to change leads, or perform any other maneuver, and it takes time and perseverance. Let the pony become familiar with the trailer before attempting a road test with forced loading. One of the best methods is to feed hay on the lowered tailgate for a few days, gradually moving the hay to the floor of the trailer; the pony, step by step, will learn to enter the now-familiar trailer of his own free will. Another method, with a green pony, is to lead him to the lowered tailgate and lift each forefoot alternately, advancing them only a few inches at a time. A slow process, to be sure, but a time-saver in the long run. Be patient, but firm, and never ask too much at any one lesson; try to end the training session while the pony is still calm, else you will have an unwelcome fight on your hands. All training at loading should be done calmly and quietly, with as few people involved as possible. Two people who know what they are doing can load any pony—any more are a hindrance. The two maxims to observe (in addition to calmness) are: keep him in the middle of the tailgate so that he cannot slip off, and make sure there is ample headroom so that he does not fear injuring his poll. Don't try to force him into a trailer that is "three-quarters of a horse tall."

If two ponies are to be loaded, put the most willing one in first; this encourages the more recalcitrant pony, who then realizes that he may be making much ado about nothing. Have hay (in net or manger) available when the pony enters the trailer; he will be more willing to load if he knows he will be rewarded with feed. Carrots or other wanted tidbits (but never sugar) can be fed during the training period to encourage the pony; do not reward the pony until he is fully loaded, haltered, and the tail chain is in place.

If you have bought a pony that resists loading, there may be a long period of retraining ahead of you before he will load quietly, particularly if he has been frightened at some time in the past. Meanwhile you may want to take him somewhere in the trailer. There is a proven method for loading a stubborn animal which is effective if done without timidity. Have the pony brought to the tailgate and faced squarely toward the opening, with a handler at his head holding the halter shank and prepared to lead forward. The handler should *not* face the pony; his job is to lead rather than indulge in a tug-of-war. When the pony has gone as far as the handler can lead him without fuss, two assistants—one stationed on each side of the pony— quickly take over by locking a hand on the other's wrist, positioning their locked arms just above the pony's hocks, and hoisting him forward.

Once the pony is loaded and the trip begun, the driver should attempt to make slowly accelerating starts and equally slow decelerations. Turns should be taken with caution; they are the principal cause of pony panic while under way. Speed is of little concern on a straightaway; there is no reason not to drive at the maximum legal limit. Upon arrival at your destination, it will probably be found that the trailer must be backed into position for unloading. To back in a given direction, the wheels must first be turned in the opposite direction (to back to the left, turn the wheel to the right) until the trailer is half-faced toward its ultimately desired position, at which point the wheels are reversed so that the car will follow the trailer. This maneuver often confuses the neophyte driver until he or she has practiced it a number of times; it will come automatically if the driver will start the back by placing only one hand on the steering wheel. With one hand grasping the wheel at its lowest point, move the hand in the direction that the trailer should move; this automatically turns the car's front wheels in the opposite direction and starts off the maneuver correctly.

GLOSSARY

ANKLE. The joint just above the hoof, technically called the fetlock.

BARN. A shelter for cattle. Horses and ponies are housed in *stables*.

BEDDING. The material placed on the floor of the stall to make the pony comfortable when lying down. There are many forms: peat moss, straw, wood shavings, and other soft, absorbent materials. Hay should never be used, as the pony will eat it and severe digestive disturbances will follow. Moldy hay can result in disaster.

BISHOPED TEETH. The deceitful practice of filing down the teeth to make the pony appear to be younger than he is. Employed by unscrupulous dealers, one of the early ones probably having the name of Bishop.

BLEMISH. An unsightliness that does not affect soundness, such as a scar.

BOTTOM LINE. The curve of the lower body in profile, between the forelegs and hind legs.

BOX. An enclosure in the stable where the pony is kept and has room to move about freely without being tied. Also known as a *box stall*.

BRIDLE. The leather contraption fitting the pony's head, to which the bit and reins are attached.

BROWSING. The eating of leaves and twigs of trees and shrubs. Eohippus, the original equine, was a browser. The domesticated pony does not browse unless he is very hungry.

BRUSHING. See INTERFERING.

CALF-KNEED. Forelegs that bow slightly to the rear, instead of being straight. A weakness that may cause the pony to break down if given hard work, and a serious conformation fault in a jumping pony.

CANTLE. The rear end of the saddle.

CAVALRY. The mounted branch of the army, now extinct in the United States. The U.S. Cavalry School at Fort Riley, Kansas, was the fountainhead of most of the wisdom in horsemanship and horse management taught today.

CAVESSON. Part of a bridle; a broad strap encircling the nose just above the bit.

CLOSE-COUPLED. Short-backed. Close-coupled ponies are generally more agile, and easier to keep in good condition, than those with long backs.

COLIC. The name for any one of several digestive disorders, all of which require the immediate attention of a veterinarian. The usual symptoms include swelling of the belly and obvious signs of internal discomfort. Keep a colicky pony on his feet and moving until help arrives. If he is allowed to lie down and roll (which very often he tries to do), he may twist an intestine.

CONFORMATION. The anatomical structure of the pony, as viewed by the observer. Good conformation is more than a thing of beauty; it indicates that the animal can perform efficiently because the component parts of the body are harmonious.

COOLER. A lightweight blanket, or heavy sheet, used after heavy exercise to help the pony "cool out."

COON-FOOTED. Term used to describe hind pasterns which slope excessively. A coon-footed pony will be comfortable to ride, but the strain on the pasterns tends to injure the ligaments during hard work. The expression derives from the way a raccoon's hind legs are joined to his feet.

COW HOCKS. Hocks that tend to point toward each other, as do a cow's, rather than being parallel. Cow-hocked ponies tend not to gallop as fast or jump as well as straight-legged ponies whose anatomy is more mechanically correct.

CREOSOTE. An evil-smelling, tar-base stain used to preserve wood. Because the taste is disliked by ponies, it makes a good preservative for stall doors, fence rails, and other projections that offer opportunities for gnawing.

CURRYCOMB. A teethed utensil used in grooming to remove scurf, dandruff, and dirt. A rubber currycomb should be applied gently over bone and other tender areas. The best use of a metal currycomb is to clean brushes.

DANDY BRUSH. A long-bristled brush held in the hand and used for grooming.

DISPOSITION. The basic temperament of the pony, as influenced by his handlers and training. He may be kindly, sulky, cooperative (willing), or indifferent. A pony with an unwilling disposition is often termed "sour," an admission that he is so because of bad handling.

DOGGY. A sarcastic reference to a lazy or stubborn pony. No slight to the canine species is intended by the user.

DUTCH DOOR. A two-part hinged stable door so constructed that the top half may be opened to admit light and air while the lower half remains closed and confines the pony to his box stall.

EASY KEEPER. A pony who thrives on normal feeding, maintaining good condition and not appearing gaunt. Close-coupled ponies are usually easier keepers than the long-bodied ones.

FEED. The pony's food, including grain, hay, and concentrated feeds.

FETLOCK. See ANKLE.

FIRING. See PINFIRING.

FOAL. A newly born pony, either male or female.

FODDER. Old-fashioned term for feed.

FORGING. Hitting the front shoe with the back shoe when in motion, usually at the trot. The blacksmith can correct forging by shortening the front toes and setting the front shoe back a trifle; this causes the pony to pick up his front feet quicker and avoid the contact. If the forging persists, the back shoes should be set farther forward, causing the pony to lift the hind feet a little later.

FOUNDER. The layman's term for *laminitis,* a disease of the foot that is extremely painful and usually incurable. There are several causes, including bad food, over-work, standing in a draft when hot, and insufficient exercise. The symptoms are lameness, heat in the wall of the foot, and a tendency for the pony to walk (if at all) as if on eggs.

FROG. The soft, horny pad in the middle of the sole of a pony's hoof. When the frog becomes hard and shriveled it must be treated, or foot problems will develop. A healthy frog touches the ground. Blacksmiths tend to overtrim frogs for cosmetic purposes; they should be restricted to trimming ragged edges.

GAIT. Any one of several sequences of placing the feet to move forward at various speeds. The pony's natural gaits are the walk, trot, and gallop. The canter is a restrained form of the gallop. The jog, or slow trot, is used to move faster than the walk and slower than the normal trot. Artificial gaits include the rack, pace, and extended trot. The amble, a natural gait for mules, is not natural to the pony. Technically, backing can be considered to be a gait.

GALVAYNE'S GROOVE. An indicator of the pony's age after about nine years, it is a well-defined vertical groove on the upper corner incisor teeth that extends gradually downward from the ninth to about the twenty-second year. By inter-polation one can estimate the pony's approximate age, but the method is not infallible.

GELDING. A male pony who has been rendered incapable of procreation. Most male ponies are gelded because unsexing makes them more tractable.

GIRTH. Sometimes referred to as the measurement of the pony's dimension around the barrel just behind the withers. The term usually denotes a broad leather strap passing under the chest and buckled to the saddle on both sides to hold it in place.

GRAIN. An important component of the pony's feed, and a necessary ingredient for building muscle and stamina. Grains include oats, corn, barley, rye, wheat, rice, and millet. However, only the first three are considered very suitable for ponies. Grain, particularly oats, can make a pony very frisky and should be fed frugally; overfeeding and underexercising can cause problems not only to the digestive system but also to the rider, who may find himself mounted on more horse than he bargained for. In England, grain is known as *corn* whereas our corn is referred to as *maize.*

GRAZING. Eating grass at liberty, as when in pasture. It is the natural means of obtaining food for wild ponies, and beneficial for the stabled pony. Wet grass can cause colic in the pony who is only occasionally pastured. The nutrients in grass are almost entirely gone by the time it turns brown.

GREEN. Term used for a pony that has had little schooling and is not a finished mount. Not so much is expected of a green pony as of an older, more experienced one.

HALTER. A device made of leather or synthetic material, similar to a bridle but without straps to secure a bit, positioned on the pony's head during periods of idleness. The main purpose of the halter is to provide an easy means of controlling the pony by hand, usually by means of a halter shank attached to a ring on the halter. Known as a *head-collar* in England.

HAND. A unit of measurement for height. A hand equals four inches, thus a fourteen-hand pony stands four feet, eight inches high. For horse show purposes, equines are divided among horses and ponies; anything more than 14.2 hands (58 inches) is a horse. Note that the figure after the decimal point is *not* a tenth but refers to the number of inches over the total hands.

HANDY. Term for an agile pony.

HAY BELLY. A swelling of the lower body behind the rib cage caused by lack of exercise combined with an almost exclusive diet of hay or grass.

HEAT. Has two definitions: (1) an increase over normal body temperature, as in an injured leg, and (2) the period when a mare is receptive to a stallion for mating purposes.

HERRING GUT. A tucked-up belly, usually found on a pony with inadequately sprung ribs. It is a conformation defect rather than a temporary physical aberration. A herring-gutted pony is seldom an easy keeper, and his bottom line makes it difficult to keep a saddle in place.

HOOF PICK. A metal device, shaped somewhat like a question mark, for cleaning the feet and lifting out stones caught in the shoe or frog. Always carry one when out riding. It should be used from heel to toe—never the other way—to avoid tearing the frog.

INTERFERING. If a pony's hind legs are not straight, but incline toward each other as they near the ground, one hoof may strike, or brush, the opposite hind leg. Normally this condition exists only at a fast trot.

IRONS. The stirrup irons, in which the feet are placed. They are usually made of aluminum or nickel, never of iron, on an "English," or flat, saddle. Most western "stock" saddles have wooden stirrups.

LEATHERS. The stirrup leathers, attaching the stirrup irons to the saddle.

LONG IN THE TOOTH. An expression of age. A pony's teeth appear to lengthen as he grows older and the gums recede, but the expression probably was intended to refer to the growth of Galvayne's groove in the tooth.

LONGE LINE. A long cotton or synthetic tape used to exercise the pony on a circle while dismounted. Pronounced "lunge."

LOOSE BOX. A box stall. So called because the pony is loose, rather than tied, when confined in it.

MANGER. A container for feed, permanently placed in the stall.

MANNERS. The pony's behavior, either well-mannered or bad-mannered. A well-mannered pony has a good disposition, and vice versa.

MARE. A female pony of four years or more. Before that she is a *filly*.

MARTINGALE. A device for restricting the pony's head while under saddle. A running martingale is Y-shaped, attaching to the girth and allowing the reins to slip through its rings at the branches of the Y. A standing martingale is a strap extending from the girth to the cavesson. An Irish martingale straps around the reins, is a nuisance, and serves merely to prevent the pony from throwing the reins over his head (which he can't do anyway, unless the rider lets go of them). A well-schooled pony does not need a martingale.

MASH. A hot bran feed given to tired ponies as a restorative and laxative.

MONDAY MORNING DISEASE. The layman's term for *azoturia,* the consequence of not cutting the amount of feed when a pony has been accustomed to hard work and enters a period of idleness (such as not being ridden over a weekend). The pony with azoturia runs a high temperature and loses control of the hindquarters. Severe cases result in death.

MUTTON WITHERS. Thick withers. A disadvantage in a riding pony because they make it difficult to keep the saddle in place.

NAVICULAR DISEASE. A serious condition, usually caused by the shock of fast work on hard ground, of the navicular bone in the hoof. Ponies with short, straight pasterns are more apt to develop navicular problems than those with the better shock-absorbing configuration of long sloping pasterns. The affliction is painful and incurable, and almost invariably confined to the forefeet. A pony who stands with his toe pointed a bit to the side, with the afflicted leg ahead of the sound leg, should be suspected of having navicular disease.

NEAR SIDE. The pony's left side. So called because most of his handling (leading, tacking up, mounting and dismounting) is done from this side.

OFF SIDE. The pony's right side.

OVER AT THE KNEE. When the pony is resting weight on a foreleg and the lower and upper leg sections (cannon bone and forearm) are not in the same vertical plane, the pony is termed "over at the knee." He appears to be preparing to kneel down. A pony with this conformation fault may be dangerous to jump, since he will be slow to bring his forelegs down at landing and hence may "peck" or even fall.

OVERREACHING. Similar to FORGING, except that the hind shoe makes contact with the foreleg above the shoe.

PADDOCK. A fenced enclosure adjacent to the stable where the pony may be turned out for rest and sunshine, but not to graze.

PASTURE. A fenced-in field, usually of several acres, where the pony is turned out to graze.

PELLETS. Any one of several brands of concentrated feed substitutes for grain and hay. While easier to handle and store, pellets do not provide the energy of good oats and are a poor substitute for hay because they do not provide the necessary roughage.

PINFIRING or FIRING. A method of applying internal heat to the knees, hocks, cannons, or fetlocks by puncturing the skin with hot needles to reduce sprain, curbs, spavins, splints, ringbone, and other deep-seated causes of lameness. Today the electric needle is used, but the procedure in the past was to use a hot iron, which was cruel and extremely painful. The pony has to be given complete rest until the hair grows back, and rest is probably the cause of the recuperation, rather than the firing. This writer advocates the rest without the firing.

PINTO. A black and white pony (a brown and white is a *skewbald*), also known as a *paint,* or *piebald*.

POMMEL. The front part of the saddle, fitting over the withers.

POMMEL PAD. An oval padding placed between the withers and an ill-fitting saddle to prevent rubbing the withers. It is better to reshape the saddle stuffing to fit the withers, and do away with the pommel pad.

POST. In equitation, a method of rising to the trot. In stable management, a post is the upright to which fence rails are attached; posts for reliable fencing should be spaced not more than eight feet apart. The best posts, virtually indestructible, are of locust.

PUREBRED. A pony whose ancestors are all of the same registered breed. The term is often confused with *thoroughbred;* there is no such thing as a thoroughbred Shetland, thoroughbred dog, and so forth.

RAIL. The horizontal part of a fence. Secure fences for a pony pasture should have at least three rails between each post.

RANK. Term used to describe a pony difficult to handle, or treacherous. A rank pony is not as bad as an outlaw, but requires the handler or rider to be alert to avoid trouble.

RATION. A normal day's supply of feed, regardless of how many times the pony is fed; it is the twenty-four-hour total, not, as frequently surmised, the total given at one feeding. Pronounced "rashun," not "rayshun."

ROACHED MANE. A mane clipped close to the neck, also referred to as a *hogged* mane.

SADDLE. The leather device placed upon the pony's back on which the rider sits. There are many types, including hacking (general riding), polo, hunting, jumping, dressage, military, racing, cow-punching, and others. Generally speaking, the "English" or flat saddle is the type used for sport and games, and the Western "stock" saddle is used for ranch work.

SAVAGING. A pony that bites with malicious intent, as opposed to taking a mere nip, is termed a savager.

SCOUR. Diarrhea, often caused by too much green feed or rich hay.

SCRAPER. A metal band or curved blade used for scraping excess sweat from the pony as an aid to drying and cooling him.

SOUND. A sound pony has no physical disabilities that will impair his ability to perform the work desired. "Hunting sound," for example, means that he is in all respects capable of putting in a good hard day following hounds cross-country.

STABLE. A permanent structure for housing ponies, sheltered from wind and rain, with stalls and feeding facilities. Without stalls, it is termed a *shed.*

STALL. The pen within which a pony is confined in the stable. There are two principal types, the BOX and the STANDING or STRAIGHT STALL.

STALLION. The mature male unaltered pony. Until the age of four he is called a *colt.* Pony stallions are usually found only at breeding farms.

STANDING STALL. See STRAIGHT STALL.

STRAIGHT STALL. A rectangular stall (as opposed to the almost square box stall) usually about 4' x 8', with provision for tying the pony to the manger.

TACK. The saddle, bridle, bit, rein, saddle blanket, and girth are all lumped together under the category of tack. "Tacking up" refers to saddling and bridling the pony.

TIED IN. A condition where the cannon bones of the forelegs are narrower just below the knee than lower down. It is a conformation fault because it denotes a weakness.

TOP LINE. The profile of the pony as observed from the poll to the base of the tail, encompassing the crest, withers, back, loin, and rump.

TRAILER. A vehicle for transporting one or more ponies that does not have its own motive power but must be towed behind a car, truck, or other vehicle.

UNSOUND. Refers to a pony that is not SOUND of wind and/or limb.

VAN. A vehicle for transporting several ponies (usually a minimum of four) that is self-propelled, as opposed to a trailer, which must be towed.

VETERINARIAN. The pony's doctor, whose word is law. It is improper to call him a veterinary, which is the name of his specialty branch of medical practice. Keep his phone number handy and call him quickly whenever there is a pony health problem that you are not absolutely certain you can cope with. Tell him the symptoms, don't attempt to diagnose the ailment.

VICE. A bad habit.

WATERING BRIDLE. Really a halter, usually made of soft rope, to which a bit can be attached by means of snaps.

WIND. The meteorologist defines wind as the movement of air and, with a pony, we are concerned with how the air moves in and out of his lungs. A breathing abnormality can be a serious defect. Good wind is developed by slow galloping but, if overdone, can result in a breakdown of the respiratory system.

WINDBREAK. Any man-made or natural feature (such as a thick stand of pine trees) behind which the pony can find protection from wind while at pasture.

SELECTED
READING

Devereux, Frederick L., Jr. *Ride Your Pony Right*. New York: Dodd, Mead & Co., 1974.

———. *Horse Problems and Problem Horses*. Old Greenwich, Conn.: Devin Adair Co., 1975.

Disston, Harry. *Know About Horses*. New York: Bramhall House, 1961.

———. *Young Horseman's Handbooks*. Charlottesville, Va.: The Jarman Press.

Saunders, George C. *Your Horse*. New York: D. Van Nostrand & Co., 1954.

Self, Margaret Cabell. *Horses: Their Selection, Care, and Handling*. New York: A. S. Barnes & Co., 1943.

Wiseman, Robert F. *The Complete Horseshoeing Guide*. Norman, Oklahoma: University of Oklahoma Press, 1968.

Woodhouse, Barbara. *The Book of Ponies*. New York: Stein and Day, 1970.

Manual of Horsemanship of the British Horse Society and the Pony Club. The British Horse Society. London.

INDEX

ABOUT
THE AUTHOR

Frederick L. Devereux, Jr. is a graduate of the famous U.S. Cavalry School at Fort Riley, Kansas. He later served as horse troop commander, horsemanship instructor at West Point, and senior judge for the American Horse Shows Association. His numerous books in the field include *Horses (A First Book)*, published by Franklin Watts, Inc. In addition to his equestrian activities he is an avid sailor and has written a book on practical navigation. Mr. Devereux lives in Vermont.